OVERCOME DEPRESSION:
STRATEGIES FROM SCIENCE AND SCRIPTURE

What People are Saying...

Margaret Lalich has written an amazing book on overcoming depression. It is deep, and yet understandable. It is well researched. It addresses the problem of depression as it touches the whole person: body, soul and spirit. It is a very practical and encouraging book about a very dark subject. I am thrilled that she has written it.

Margaret has been in the trenches, both professionally and personally. She doesn't write theoretically from an ivory tower, but from the place of walking with others as they fight off the "black dog" of depression.

Pastor Bill Walden
Cornerstone Ministries, Napa, CA

Margaret Lalich's research, experience and reflections are beautifully interwoven to create this resource on overcoming depression. Be inspired that this timely topic can be conquered in the light of Scriptures and relevant suggestions presented here.

Pastor Ryan Escobar
Christ's Commission Fellowship, New Zealand

OVERCOME DEPRESSION
Strategies from Science & Scripture

MARGARET LALICH, M.S., M.A.

STONEWORKS MEDIA
Napa, California

PUBLISHED BY STONEWORKS MEDIA PUBLISHING
952 School Street #103, Napa, CA. 94559

DISCLAIMER

The opinions shared here do not necessarily represent those of any employer, company, or organization that I am affiliated with. All content in this book (text, images, audio, or other formats), were created for information purposes only. It is not intended to be a substitute for professional medical, psychiatric, psychological advice, diagnosis, or treatment.

Always seek the advice of your physician or other qualified health provider with any questions you may have regarding medical conditions. Never disregard professional advice or delay in seeking it because of something you have read in this, or any other, self-help resource.

The information provided is based on interpretation of research findings, and literature, as well as professional and personal experience. I am standing on the shoulders of giants as I offer this work. I do so with gratitude. I have made every effort to assure it, but make no representations as to accuracy, completeness, currency, suitability, or validity of any information—and will not be liable for any errors, omissions, or delays in this information.

If you gain benefit from this book, please leave a review on the bookstore website where you purchased it. Thank you.

Printed in the United States of America
First Edition: March 2019

Lalich, Margaret
Overcome Depression: Strategies from Science & Scripture
ISBN 978-1-7329874-0-1

Cover and book design by Andrew Benzie
www.andrewbenziebooks.com

*This book is dedicated (in memory) to my husband Joseph Lalich,
my partner, and best friend...
and to the readers who give it meaning by using this work
in their own recovery—to the glory of God.*

CONTENTS

PART ONE: BRAIN SCIENCE

>   Depression is not a sin. Find hope, help, strategies,
>   and the reasons for them.

>   A reader-friendly introduction: Neuro-anatomy and physiology.
>   We can map and navigate.

>   The neural-network: electro-chemical balance, pathways,
>   power grids and engineering abilities.

>   Our *use-it-or-lose-it* design. Explores the brain/body connection,
>   and how to use its power.

>   Our God-given tri-level brain design and operation.
>   We *choose* which levels to cruise.

>   The Brain's R.A.S. regulates traffic *(100,000,000 impulses per sec.)*.
>   *We* set *its* control.

>   Brain circuitry, and organization: The power of collaboration.
>   We are resource managers.

>   Brain regeneration: Neurogenesis, and our role in it..

PART TWO: MIND MATTERS

PART THREE: BODY TALK

FOREWORD

by Karl Benzio, M.D.

L et me ask you an interesting question: What do you get when you combine the skills and expertise of a Counselor and Physician? That would be a Psychiatrist. Now let me ask you an even more intriguing question? Who does the Bible describe as the Wonderful Counselor and Great Physician? Jesus! Yes, that makes Jesus the Perfect Psychiatrist.

Jesus came to earth for many reasons, but I believe the main reason Jesus came down to earth was to start a Behavioral Health Revolution! Don't believe me? Then let's look at what He actually said:

Luke 4, tells of Jesus' teaching in the synagogue from Isaiah 61:

He will come to heal the broken-hearted (meaning the depressed or psychologically struggling), and set the captives free—those enslaved in their own psychological shackles or prisons or with walls formed by addictive substances, destructive thought patterns, feelings, fears, or behaviors.

In John 10:10, Jesus states: The thief comes to steal, kill, and destroy. I came that they may have life, and have it abundantly.

In Mark 2:16-17, Jesus clarified (for the confused, old-guard-mentality Pharisees) what His purpose really was: "And the scribes of the Pharisees, when they saw that he was eating with sinners and tax collectors, said to his disciples, 'Why does he eat with tax collectors and sinners?' When Jesus heard it, he said to them, "Those who are well have no need of a physician, but those who are sick need one. I came not to heal the righteous, but came to heal the sinners."

Jesus' ultimate goal is our psycho-spiritual healing… in eternity for sure, but He also desires to heal us in our earthly life (for me on earth from 1963 to death). I am talking about a healing which delivers the true desires of our heart—peace, joy, purpose, value, un-conditional love, acceptance, belonging, forgiveness, passion, meaning, safety, security, order, and direction. This amazing and truly miraculous healing happens when we apply Jesus' teachings. This is the abundant life Jesus taught, role modeled, and died to give us.

Even though the Bible reveals many psychological teachings and principles, and Jesus taught His revolutionary, countercultural, yet simple psychological prescription for healing—sadly, many Christians, (and the Church) have a hard time accepting, engaging, or receiving help from psychiatrists and psychology.

I've treated thousands of patients over 30 years, and believe the main reason for this fear of psychiatry/psychology is our incredible lack of understanding of our mind. God's most amazing creation is the human mind. We can't even come close to replicating or imitating it. And like any good inventor, God wants you to get the most use and enjoyment out of this amazing creation. Good creators, inventors, and manufacturers don't make you guess how to get the most out of their inventions. They provide an instruction manual.

God gave us the perfect instruction manual for how to use our mind for maximum satisfaction and abundant living. The Best Instruction Book for Living Everyday (the B.I.B.L.E.) is the most accurate Psychiatric textbook ever written. It is the most accurate revelation of what goes on inside our mind, why we struggle, and how the mind is healed.

For most people, the mind is mysterious, overwhelming, frightening, and at times crippling. In this text, Margaret successfully pulls back the curtain to clearly and simply reveal how our mind works. She uses simple word pictures and easy vocabulary to not just reduce the mystery, but also helps us realize how to use this powerful mind to our advantage instead of just using it to get in more trouble. Margaret then uses her experience and awesome ability to take the next step and show us how to simply, but powerfully, blend this understanding of the mind with biblical instruction and principles to equip us with some easy and practical skills. Like any skills, the more we practice, the better we get at them.

Our lives go in the direction of our decisions. Make Godly decisions, and our life goes well. Make decisions that are not consistent with Godly teaching, and life is a lot harder with much anxiety, sadness, and hurt. Psychology is just the understanding of why we do what we do, or why we make the decisions we make. This life-changing book shows us how to use psychology to implement the great instruction of the BIBLE so we can be not just hearers of the word, but actual doers. May you be blessed as you open and engage this fun and eye-opening resource to unleash the power of the Holy Spirit to renew your mind, transform your life and achieve the psycho-spiritual healing Jesus wants to bless you with.

Karl Benzio, M.D.
Medical Director, Honey Lake Clinic
Founder and Clinical Director, Lighthouse Network
Pennsylvania Director, American Academy of Medical Ethics
Addiction and Counseling HELPLINE:
    844-Life-Change (844-543-3242)

CHAPTER 1—FIRST THINGS FIRST: CHRISTIANS AND DEPRESSION

"For God has not given us a spirit of fear, but of power and of love and of a sound mind." 2 Timothy 1:7

C*hurch is not a museum for perfect saints—it's a first aid station for sinners who keep trying.* I can't recall the name of the pastor, who delivered that line, but his message resonated with me then and it still does today. I want to contribute to First-Aid supplies.

God says He is for us, and we are loved. We can trust, and we must believe His Word. But, it can be hard to reconcile faith with depression, anxiety or other mental health issues. If you have struggled with this—you're not alone. Right from the start, you need to know you are loved. We're in this together.

Doubts and fears can seed questions such as:

"What's happening?"

"Why?"

"Now what?"

If you ask these questions, be assured God hears the cry of your heart. By His grace, we will explore answers together. Yes, there are answers. Yes, there is hope and help that you can use—right where you are, starting now.

WHAT'S IT ALL ABOUT?

There has been a revolution in the study of the brain (neuroscience). We've started to understand brain-works, and can now answer the first of our opening questions: "What's happening?" With today's technology and new imaging systems we can see the brain in action as thoughts, and new learning, form physical links, creating neural patterns and pathways within the brain.

The glory of God is revealed as we discover more of His divine design, and watch new scientific findings align with the old wisdom of God's word for mankind. Proverbs 23:7 says: "For as he thinks in his heart, so he is." We have learned that what we *think* helps to form who, and what we are. We can use this knowledge to build recovery skills.

This book is a resource for faith-based self-help. It is not intended to replace professional treatment, but to offer more information and coping skills for independent use. It is not psychotherapy. It *is* skill building. The skills presented here do not present a 'cure' for depression—only God can offer healing. They *will* help light pathways to recovery.

In this text you will find brain science, powerful and practical recovery strategies, evidence-based therapies, and scriptures you can use to ease the grip of depression and anxiety. Mood disorders affect the whole person. We will build recovery skills in four major areas including Biological, Psychological, Social, and Spiritual dimensions. Information is based on current research, clinical practice, and personal experience.

Study of brain science might seem far removed from the practical strategies we are eager to explore, but it's important, and it will pay off. Reaching any goal requires commitment. If you want to win the Daytona 500, you must first learn to operate your vehicle, and then drive, baby, drive!

WHY I WANT TO SHARE WITH YOU

I believe we are blessed—so that we can *be* a blessing to others. I'm a believer, a writer, a speech-language pathologist, and an education specialist. I have more than 30 years of experience, working with patients who have had to deal with some of the same issues that may be plaguing you.

My work has included collaborative curriculum development and the teaching of various mental health recovery skills. My students were patients/residents in a secured, state mental hospital. Most found themselves in trouble with the law for actions taken while in the grip of mental illnesses. All were seeking or were already on, a path to recovery. Many walked that path right through the high, razor-wired security gates, to rejoin their families and society.

I've been blessed to share their stories, to walk with them through some of their struggles, and to celebrate with many, as they stepped out of despair into the light of hope. We tried hands-on, practical strategies for coping with depression, anxiety and other symptoms of mental illnesses. We discovered; Failure isn't fatal—it's educational.

I'm not a psychiatrist or psychologist. I don't diagnose or treat illnesses, or prescribe medications. Thank God that professional counsel, therapeutic treatment, and medications are available. I hope those in need don't hesitate to seek them. And, by God's grace, there is much that individuals can do for themselves, with powerful, evidence-based self-help tools.

At the hospital, I could not share matters of faith, because of constraints governing presentations within a state-run facility. This text is not so limited. We will take full advantage of the truth offered in 2nd. Timothy 3:16 "All scripture is given by inspiration of God and is profitable...." All Bible references will be from the New King James Version (NKJV) unless noted otherwise.

A FEW WORDS ABOUT CONTENT

When I'm learning a new skill, I ask…, "How does a thing like that work?" It helps me to "get it" when I understand the reasoning behind a skill set. It also boosts my confidence, and my motivation, to know there actually *are* reasons.

How about you? After absorbing new information, I also ask, "So what? " "How can I use this?" and "What's the cost or benefit?" We will seek answers together.

FIRST THINGS FIRST

One of the first things we must do is to get rid of judgment. Depression, Anxiety, or mental illnesses are not crimes or sins. Yes, at times sin, (even crime) might be part of the picture—before, during, or after a struggle with this calamity. But the problems, themselves, are not. Too often we waste our strength and energy on thoughts like these:

> "If I had real faith, I could beat this thing."
> "If God is for me—why do I feel like such a loser?"
> "What kind of sin have I committed to deserve this?"
> "What's the matter with me? I'm so ashamed."

Does any of that sound familiar? It's sad that we say such things to ourselves. And, we fear that others are thinking these same, and even worse, things about us. Maybe some are. But if they are, it shows their own lack of understanding, not proof of our guilt or failure. Fear of what others are thinking or saying is one of the major hurdles we must overcome. We can't afford to let shame stop us, or anyone else, from asking for, and receiving help.

Jesus spent most of His time and energy with those who were in trouble. I love His response when He was questioned about people He associated with… 'when Jesus heard that, He said to them: *Those who are well have no need of a physician, but those who are sick.*" Matthew 9:12

As for judging ourselves—it is written: "There is therefore now no condemnation to those who are in Christ Jesus, who do not walk according to the flesh, but according to the Spirit." Romans 8:1

SOMETHING TO THINK ABOUT

The National Alliance on Mental Illness, and volumes of research says that depression is one of the most successfully treated conditions (80% relief). Yet the majority who experience depression and anxiety don't seek help. Why? If lack of knowledge is the reason, we need to learn together. If it's because of fear, or embarrassment, we need to encourage each other to boldly seek the help we need.

If a friend with Cancer did not seek treatment (with traditional or alternative medicines, diet, surgery or some other therapy), we'd think they should try *something*. We'd argue against waiting for the Cancer to run its course, out of fear that to seek treatment would admit to being weak in faith. We'd be upset knowing such an approach to Cancer is dangerous and could be fatal. Left untreated, depression and anxiety can be equally dangerous. Sadly, many slip into thinking of suicide as their only option.

Suicide is a terrible loss for us all. It happens far too often because someone felt alone, lost hope or couldn't imagine any other solution to a problem or a way to end the pain. And we weren't given (or didn't recognize); the opportunity to share some of our own hope, or to remind them they are not alone, and that there are other options.

WHAT CHOICES DO WE HAVE?

No one chooses to feel bad, right? Right. There is no blame here. Life is choice. Love is a choice. Recovery depends, in large measure, on choice. We have free will. Our God said we must 'choose' the way we will go. But, what if we don't know which choice to make, or even what choices are possible?

Courage! There are options. The problem is how easily we lose sight of them. As we stand in depression's shadow, we may doubt the very *existence* of light. We can hardly imagine choosing to search for it.

Even in the darkest depression—light exists. Believe it!

If you can't find that faith in yourself right now, hang on to the word of God, and be encouraged. He, Himself, *is* light. When you're feeling lost and very far from God, and you fear you can't find Him, be assured that He knows right where you are.

LIFE IN THE SHADOWLANDS

Major depression can feel like falling into a dark emotional pit. The moment of falling—right then—is when we need to forcefully declare, "If there are shadows, there must be light." Hang on to that truth. Say it out loud. Let it reassure you.

Only light can cast shadows. Since that's a provable fact, then as sad/bad as they appear, shadows are proof that light exists, even if we can't, immediately, see the source of it. John 8:12 says; "Then Jesus spoke to them again, saying, *I am the light of the world. He who follows Me shall not walk in darkness, but have the light of life."*

If you doubt that you have enough faith to believe, please know, you don't have to believe in the strength or power of your own faith. It's Jesus we must believe in. We can trust Him, even when we doubt, even when we're afraid, and even if we don't feel faithful. As scripture records: " If we are faithless, He remains faithful; He cannot deny Himself" (2 Timothy 2:13). We may fail, but He cannot deny His own character.

We may feel isolated as if we were alone at the end of the world, but the world keeps right on spinning, and we are still part of it (even if we're reeling). We can only see shadows when we look away from the light. This is a beautiful, but double-edged, truth. It offers hope we can hold on to, but it can also cut to the heart if used to blame the person who is depressed. Please don't blame yourself, or others. Refocus.

Like Peter, walking on water, we instantly sink when we look away from our Lord to focus on our storms or shadows. Such distraction is completely human. Also, like Peter, we will feel the Lord's saving grasp when we cry for help. See Matthew 14:28-31.

PLAYING THE BLAME GAME

Blame is a distraction. We cast blame on ourselves with hurtful thinking when we think or say things like: "If I had enough faith this wouldn't happen." Or, " I should be stronger… blah, blah, blah."

Don't surrender to this way of thinking. Stop it, and take corrective action. Believe it or not, we can often command this internal voice to be still, by shouting, "Stop!" Try it. Shout out loud, or even inside your own head. Then remind yourself the God of heaven created you. Ask for His help. He loves you beyond measure.

Our God doesn't make junk. He says you are His special treasure. Use your favorite Gospel Bible verses to affirm these truths. Try repeating them, out loud. God's word, in your voice, can drown doubt, and silence hurtful self-talk.

Sometimes blame is accidentally dished out by well-meaning friends or loved ones who want to help 'fix' the problem. It can come with sentiments that sound a lot like the beatings we just gave ourselves, such as "It can't be that bad," "Get a grip," "Cheer up," "Count your blessings," "You'll be fine," and "Where is your faith?"

Friends and family usually don't mean to minimize our pain or to cause injury. These things may be said with the best of intentions. Repeat after me: There are NO winners in the blame game (whether blaming ourselves or others). Counting our blessings is always a good idea, and we may need added support too.

SPACE—THE FINAL FRONTIER

In a cosmic analogy, depression shares characteristics of a black hole. Black holes exist in deep space. This invisible 'dark matter' may be approached from a distance without notice, but with great risk. Straying too close leads to entrapment. The movie *Interstellar* introduced us to the concept of an "event horizon." It's the point of no return. Science has proposed the gravity of a black hole is so strong that not even light can escape.

In the past, we theorized that anything falling into a black hole was doomed to stay forever. But one of our greatest scientific minds (Steven Hawking) has disputed that idea. Explaining "Hawking Radiation," he suggested that black holes could shrink and die, with loss of trapped matter. These emissions (small energy fluctuations, near the event horizon in space) form the 'radiation' he wrote of.

Hawking concluded: "The message of this lecture is, that black holes ain't as black as they are painted. They are not the eternal prisons they were once thought. Things can get out of a black hole, both to the outside and, possibly, to another universe." Any escaping particles would be profoundly changed by the experience.

Depression can also be approached with great risk. Moods can shift in small stages until we slip too close and fall into a black hole. In the grip of this disastrous emotion, we too may feel there is no escape. We can't afford to give in to this unproven fear. We are better advised to recall Steven Hawking's conclusion about the physical universe and apply it to our own experience. He said, "So if you feel you are in a black hole, don't give up. There's a way out."

We will explore some ways of escape together, and we too may be profoundly changed by the experience.

While outer-space exploration claims the headlines, inner space (within our own minds) offers the greatest frontier for life-changing discovery. God's creative genius and His generosity are on full display in the majesty of His creation. Knowledge is power, and we're about to turn it on. All set for space exploration?

Get ready to launch!

PART ONE:
BRAIN SCIENCE

This book is designed in three parts, to cover all dimensions of depression as it affects the whole person through Biology, Psychology, and Social domains. The three book parts include:

1. Brain Science
2. Mind Matters
3. Body Talk

Scriptures weave through all sections. They are the ties that support and bind the whole together and offer a deeper understanding. Scripture lights up the content, in sometimes surprising ways, with the application of age-old wisdom to new scientific breakthroughs.

I often use word-picture analogies and metaphor to offer simplified, meaningful illustrations of complex subjects. This helps me to grasp ideas and reach a deeper understanding. I pray the same for you. My goal is to be clear and reader-friendly.

Inner Space is exciting and we can learn to navigate with more effective power than we may have recognized before. Welcome to Neuro-Theology and to the inner-space-territory of your own brain/mind.

CHAPTER 2—BLAST OFF!
TO INNER SPACE

Have you noticed if you focus your gaze on a single object it seems to grow while other things shrink into the background? Hyper-focus can cause distortion.

This may help to explain 16th-century man's confusion. He could see the rising and setting of the Sun and Moon as they crossed the fixed, flat line of the horizon. He felt no movement as his view of the night sky filled with stars, wheeling across the sky. Based on his own sensory experience, he believed the universe rotated around our, obviously flat, earth. Men gazed at the nighttime heavens and were filled with great wonder but little understanding.

Galileo built his first telescope in 1609. After discovering the four largest moons of Jupiter, sunspots, and the phases of Venus, he concluded that all planets revolved around the Sun, and, like the Earth itself, they rotated on their own axis. His report was heresy to men who believed that *we* were at the center of the galaxy, and everything revolved around us. At times, we might make new versions of that same mistake. Making ourselves the center of all things distorts, and can block our view of a universe full of potential.

Since the 16th century we've taken to the sky, orbited the earth, landed on the Moon, and are excitedly planning journeys to Mars. *Star Trek*, a classic TV series, declared our mission to: "...Boldly Go Where No one Has Gone Before."

I'm a fan of space exploration and study of our universe. The more we learn, the more we can appreciate divine design, and recognize and understand the incredible, interactive detail of God's glorious creation.

As exciting as outer space exploration is, I am even more awed and "star-struck" by the universe of Inner Space. The same God whose artistry created outer space created His most intimate art in His own image. That's you and me.

WHAT IS INNER SPACE?

Inner space is between our ears. It is where the seeds of thoughts, beliefs, and decisions grow. It's the strike point for the sparks that set our physical, mental, and emotional lives in motion. As with any discovery, the more we learn and understand—the more we can appreciate the designer's hand. We can learn the dimensions of this space. We can find and learn to use, landmarks to guide our growth and journey towards recovery.

SCIENCE MEASURES INNER SPACE

The average human brain weighs just about three pounds, which is the size of a small head of cabbage. Inside the human brain we have about one hundred billion brain cells. One hundred billion is also the estimated number of stars in the Milky Way Galaxy.

Each of those brain cell neurons has an axon (a length of connecting fiber), and dendrites (shorter branches of connecting nerve fiber). Axons are the wiring used by the brain cell to send signals from one neuron to another. Dendrites receive and relay these signals.

Research reports each brain cell neuron can connect with ten thousand other neurons, and make up to two-hundred thousand dendrite connections through the nerve fibers. These fibers range from a few millimeters, up to several feet in length. It's been suggested that there might be ten thousand miles of fiber network within one cubic inch of neo-cortex tissue. However, to know for sure we'd have the impossible job of un-stacking, straightening and smoothing these fibers for measurement.

As we consider the sheer volume of our nerve fiber wiring, keep this verse in mind: "Are not two sparrows sold for a copper coin? And not one of them falls to the ground apart from your Father's will. But the very hairs of your head are all numbered. Do not fear therefore; you are of more value than many sparrows." Matthew 10:29-31

Each axon and dendrite is many times finer than a single hair, which God has individually counted. Imagine how much more He is aware of and cares about, these strands within inner space, which conduct the impulses of our very lives.

THINK ABOUT THE POTENTIAL

We have one hundred billion neurons, each capable of connecting with ten thousand others, and of receiving signals from up to 200,000 dendritic connections (traveling over thousands of miles of our neural network), all folded and wrapped within our three-pound "brain-universe." Now that's potential!

The numbers are almost too big to seem real. They stagger me. They also excite me, because every bit of connectivity creates new possibility. Our thoughts form our connections and the connections are the substance of our lives. It's all part of God's grand design for us. He is aware of every detail, and of how each of the smallest parts of His design is working.

In the Old Testament, King David put it this way: "How precious also are Your thoughts to me, O God! How great is the sum of them! If I should count them, they would be more in number than the sand; When I awake, I am still with You." (Psalms 139:17-18).

Knowledge is power. Once we clearly outline the territory, we can learn to map and navigate the internal network of brain cells, and patterns of connections, which are called neural pathways. When we understand how these connections are made, we can discover the impact of our God-given power. We can then use it to develop our own very personal "information highways." What we may not have realized is that we can revise these highway routes, chart new courses and indeed, "Boldly Go" by the grace of God.

STRATEGIES

There are power strategies you can use to explore your own inner space. Here are a few of them:

START A JOURNAL

At this beginning stage write down points of particular interest in what you read. Write questions you still have and verses that you find especially meaningful. Leave room as you write to jot down answers and references as we discover them. Your journal will become a personal treasure if you start now to make it a part of your experience with this study.

STARGAZE

Pick a safe spot for stargazing tonight. Get out in the fresh air and look up. With the naked eye, we can see more stars than we can count, and remember, the estimated one hundred billion stars contained within the Milky Way Galaxy is the same best "guesstimate" number of brain cells within your personal inner space.

The same God who placed the Sun and Moon in the heavens is also credited with this: "He counts the number of stars; He calls them all by name." Psalms 147:4

The One who knows every star by name also knows *your* name. He holds all things in His hands—including the universe and you, and me.

SCRIPTURES FOR MEDITATION

"When I consider Your heavens, the work of Your fingers, The moon and the stars, which You have ordained; What is man that You are mindful of him, And the son of man that You visit him? For You have made him a little lower than the angels, And You have crowned him with glory and honor. You have made him to have dominion over the works of your hands; You have put all things under his feet, all sheep and oxen, even the beasts of the field, the birds of the air, and the fish of the sea, that pass through the paths of the seas. O Lord, our Lord, How excellent is Your name in all the earth!" Psalms 8:3-9

As you read this Psalm, notice the part that says: "You have made him (mankind) to have dominion over the works of your hands." Note that *we are also works of His hands.*

Our God has given us power over our own systems that we may not yet realize we have. Many people don't seem to be aware of the treasures they have or the treasures they, themselves, are.

Dear reader, God treasures you just as you are. He has even more love and treasure He wants to lavish on us.

In the next chapter, we will learn more about His works, as we zoom in for a close up view of basic 'brain network' operations. It's positively electrifying!

CHAPTER 3—LIVE WIRES: 'BABY, YOU'RE HOT'!

This is not an anatomy textbook, but investing your time and energy to understand the systems and operations of "inner space" will pay great dividends.

Like those Daytona 500 drivers, we have operating instructions and strategies to master, as we enter our own race and want to win the prize of recovery.

You can have a winning strategy for coping with depression and anxiety. There are skills that work—and reasons that they do. We can learn to use them.

OUR POWER GRID

As we know, connections in the brain are wired into thousands of miles of nerve fiber. These 'live' wires form the neural network.

At the heart of each neuron, all of the action is electrical. Each impulse is a spark from "brain-cell central." When enough sparks hit a neuron it fires and, sends the signal to the end of its axon. These signals trigger the release of chemicals called neurotransmitters. They, flow across the "synaptic gap" (imagine a gap in a spark plug in a race car engine), and are then received by adjoining brain cell neurons.

Each synaptic receptacle is uniquely designed to admit a single specific neurotransmitter, like a chemical lock and key. These chemical stimulations trigger new sparks which speed along axons for transfer. Sparks hit the center of the receiving cell with a fresh electrical impulse, and the beat goes on.

From cell-to-cell, it's a complex exchange that happens with incredible speed, and without our deliberate help, millions of times a day.

Every time we learn something new, or seriously ponder something in a new way, we challenge the brain to create new neural connections. Everything we learn links to everything we already know. Our thoughts form new connections. We can map new learning by looking at the physical links that are formed between brain cells. Yes, brain scans actually show these physical links.

THE ELECTRO-CHEMICAL NETWORK

Connections between neurons are tenuous at first, but as we continue to use them, they build strength and bulk up much like the muscles of a body-builder. Patterns of connection are called neural pathways. That term describes the union of brain cells firing together to accomplish specific physical and mental tasks.

When a learning, or thinking, challenge is met and repeated, this union of brain cells becomes wired together in a routine of specific performance. With each repetition, connections get stronger, and communication is enhanced with faster and smoother transmission of signals, speeding along a well-developed and well-traveled path.

Just as our neural pathways increase in strength and size with use, they will weaken and dissolve if they are not used. These connections atrophy, just as muscles do, if not exercised. We have a use-it-or-lose-it design.

NETWORK EXPANSION AND INTEGRATION

Some parts of the body don't connect directly with the brain's neural network of live wires, yet information travels efficiently outside of the wired neural network too. Signals go to and from the brain through every inch of our beings. It's a fully integrated system.

While chemistry carries signals from one cell to another, across the gap at the synapse within the brain, it uses the blood stream and cerebrospinal fluid to ferry signals through other parts of the body in a process called Chemo-taxis. That word means that the chemical "ferries" itself. Each chemical signal carries neurotransmitters, combined with other peptides and steroids, to form discreet messages, which orchestrate our lives.

We recognize the names of some commonly known neurotransmitters: Adrenaline, Cortisol, Serotonin, Dopamine, Epinephrine, and Norepinephrine, are among the most familiar. But there are still hundreds more that we know of, and more yet to be discovered. Too much, or too little, of any ingredient in this fabulous flow can cause a chemical imbalance—which spells trouble for us.

Remember, that all of the action within the neuron is electrical, and the action between brain cells (and throughout the other parts of the body), is chemical. As we begin to explore the power of choice, it is critical to understand how important chemistry is to that transmission of mental "current" throughout our synaptic neural networks, and for the rest of the body.

THE POWER OF CHOICE

Our thinking patterns, and decisions to challenge the brain with new learning develop our connections and pathways. The way we handle emotions, and choose to order our lives impacts the quantity and strengths of connections we can make, and the chemical balance we need for effective electrical/chemical transmission.

This may seem like heavy responsibility at a time when you'd like your burdens to be lighter. But take heart. This is actually good news because responsibility, in this case, also means opportunity. Our choices have power.

For now, just keep reading. Give yourself credit for choosing to make consistent recovery efforts, even when, or especially when, you don't feel up to it. Acknowledge your progress. You are making a good, informed choice by taking the time to learn about, and become mindful of, your own "inner space." You will find gifts within.

What a God! We are His design, and He cares about each of the billions of intricate operations, every bit of wiring in the network, every connection, and each neural pathway in our brains— every single thought, at every single second, of every single day. He's paying attention to every detail. He said so! "For the ways of man are before the eyes of the Lord, And He ponders all his paths." Proverbs 5:21

STRATEGIES

Knowledge is power, but knowledge alone is not enough. We must take action.

CONSIDER YOUR CHEMISTRY

We can take better note of what we're feeding our (brains both physically and mentally). Hmmm, my drugs of choice could be carbs or chocolate. What are yours?

Stimulants and tranquilizers are chemicals too. So, be mindful of things like excess caffeine, sugar, and other kinds of stimulating or tranquilizing substances we consume. Experiment, and take note of the effects. Write them down.

Over The Counter (OTC) remedies, and supplements, can also affect the balance in brain chemistry in a big way. Use caution. "When In Doubt, Check It Out." Ask your health practitioner or nutritionist.

HORMONES ARE CHEMICALS TOO

Hormones are some of the most powerful chemicals to affect our brains and bodies. They operate internally, but many are subject to external control too. For example, Adrenaline and Cortisol are two well-known stress hormones.

In balance, they work as designed for our protection. In excess, they can be destructive, leading to distress and disease.

We can affect the release of these two powerful neurotransmitters by staying aware of our own stress and responding as quickly as possible to reduce it when we notice elevated levels.

BREATHE FOR STRESS CONTROL

A few deep breaths can change brain chemistry quickly. To relieve stress, try inhaling through your nose, to a slow count of four, and then hold it for a four-count, before releasing that breath. Exhale through your mouth to another slow count of four.

When you exhale, let the air pass between your lips as if blowing out a candle. Note: Because of our body design, deep inhalation should cause your stomach to push out. It will move in (relaxed again) when you exhale. If your shoulders rise as you inhale, you aren't getting a deep and relaxed diaphragmatic breath. Try again.

. For even deeper inhalation, try a wide, deliberate smile as you relax. Sit or stand tall, and take that breath in. A big smile can change the airway, and can positively affect brain chemistry/mood. Try for at least four or five of these slow, deep breaths. Ten is even better.

CHECK WHAT YOU EAT

Dr. Daniel Amen, M.D., a noted clinical neuroscientist and psychiatrist, suggests that what is good for our hearts is also good for our brains. Keep this in mind when planning menus.

CONTACT

Even if it's a short S.O.S, all prayer is a Godly connection. Making contact, whether or not we feel a response, reminds us that we are not alone. Our God is with us, and He is able to handle what concerns us each moment of every day. That deep breath and "S.O.S." prayer can happen simultaneously. They work well together.

WALK IT OFF

Movement is powerful and can help us think.

DEVELOP A HABIT OF PRAISE

Praise is the quick-connect to the highest power we can reach. It might be hard in a given circumstance, but praise God anyway—no matter what. It takes effort, but we can do it. Like King David, we can recognize music as a power tool. If you have a favorite praise/worship tune, turn it on and crank it up.

MAINTAIN A JOURNAL

What was most interesting for you in this chapter? If you tried some of the strategies, and I hope you did, what was your result? Do you have more questions? Write them down.

We will find answers together.

SCRIPTURE FOR MEDITATION

"I will call upon the Lord, who is worthy to be praised; So shall I be saved from my enemies." 2 Samuel 22:504

There is much more to come. Be encouraged!

CHAPTER 4—INNER SPACE TRAVEL ADVISORY

We would stand amazed if we had an inside view of our brain activity. As electrical sparks at the center of each brain cell send impulses down the axon lines to be received, then relayed by dendrites, those sparks of life create a fabulous light show.

Electrical power lines need insulation. Axons are coated with myelin, a fatty substance that wraps the axon in link-sausage-shaped sections to serve this purpose. The thicker the layer of myelin, the more efficient signal transmission becomes.

This insulating sheath allows electrical impulses to leap down the axon from link to link, or as scientists say, from (node to node). Think of these leaps as short cuts, so that signals don't have to travel through every millimeter (through thousands of miles) of fiber on their way down neural pathways.

The speed of transmission is incredible. Signals can travel along un-insulated nerve fibers at approximately one meter per second. With healthy myelin insulation, transmission speeds can reach one hundred meters per second. Flawed development or damage to the myelin sheath can disrupt the efficient flow of signals.

RISK REDUCTION

Electrochemical science is interesting, and it has life-changing significance. What goes into our bodies will affect our brains—from before birth, and through adulthood. For example, Fetal Alcohol Spectrum Disorder, and adult alcoholism present real dangers to our systems.

Damage to insulation is commonly caused by disease, or viral inflammation. Vascular disease or damage (stroke) can injure myelin and more. Traumatic brain injury, or a stroke may cause the death or damage of brain cells (neurons). Neural connections can be broken through accidental twisting or shearing of axons and dendrites or via damage-related roadblocks.

PERSONAL POWER

Dramatic as they are, developmental problems, disease, and trauma are not the only cause of loss and injury for the neural network. We have a use-it-or-lose-it design. Neglect can weaken the network, or dissolve its structure, connections, and insulation. One of the most exciting areas of recent discovery is the amount of control we have in this magnificent system.

Neural connections are made when we challenge the brain with thinking. Here is some good Old Testament advice: "Ponder the path of your feet, and let all your ways be established." Proverbs 4:26

As we think deeply, or master new skills, pathways are established, with physical links, between brain cells. These connections may be weak at first. They bulk up and get stronger with use. As we continue to challenge our minds, and engage in repeated practice, we add new layers of myelination. This continues to increase the efficiency of signal transmission, and the strength of brain cell connections.

Travel is faster and steps more sure as we maintain and develop neural pathways with use. If we stop using them, our insulation shrinks, and connections weaken and dissolve over time. They can vanish with neglect, much like unused footpaths through a jungle disappear as they are reclaimed. Yes, sometimes my thoughts can resemble a jungle—*wild*. How about you?

May God help us make the right connections, and to keep our pathways clear.

Our food, drinks, and drug menus, our levels of mental activity, and our emotional choices all can, and will, impact how our systems work. Changes in the chemical balance in our brains increase its vulnerability in very real ways.

MIND AND MATTER

Are our brains and our minds the same thing? The brain is a physical organ of the body. The mind is consciousness and the foundation of our thoughts, beliefs, and emotions. Can we have one without the other? These two parts of our beings are intimately connected, and both link to the body as well. We may not always be aware of our mind/body influences, but they do not operate separately, unless one is in a coma (and we aren't one hundred percent certain, even then).

What we put into our bodies, and how we use them, significantly affects our minds. Our minds also have an impact on our bodies. It works both ways. This can be good news, or bad, depending on what we do with the knowledge.

If you doubt your power—try this:

Imagine spotting a police car right behind you on the freeway. Try to visualize it. He came out of no-where and just suddenly appeared in your rear-view mirror. He hits the lights and siren. Maybe he's targeting you, or he may be clearing a path through traffic, attempting to get by you to attend to something else up ahead. Notice your body's instant response. Your eyes will dart to the speedometer. Your foot will ease up (or press down) on the gas pedal. Your heart rate will probably increase. Your face may flush. You might notice sweaty or shaky hands. Your breathing rate may change. Muscles tense. Your stomach may suddenly feel bottomless. It's a visceral reaction. This is an example of how your mind triggers physical reactions.

Want more examples? Imagine the mouth-watering aroma of baking cinnamon rolls. Consider the sensations aroused by close whispers from a loved one's lips. Think of the way you respond to different sounds and rhythms of music. These are all physical responses to mental (sensory) activity generated by your mind. You imagined them into being. That's power!

The body/mind communication of our system holds great promise. Since it is two-way, we can build real strategies and tap into this strength, to make things work better and help ourselves get through tough experiences. It's all made possible because of our incredible, divine design.

God is the ultimate architect and designer. He allows us to work with His blueprint. Don't worry, He provides the help, training, and skills we will need, just as He did when designing His Jerusalem temple.

Exodus 35: 31-33 says, "…and He has filled him with the Spirit of God, in wisdom and understanding, in knowledge and all manner of workmanship, to design artistic works, to work in gold and silver and bronze, in cutting jewels for setting, in carving wood, and to work in all manner of artistic workmanship." Exodus 35: 31-33

Elsewhere in scripture, we read that *we* are living temples of God. We can be sure He has plans, just as magnificently detailed, for our living temples, as He did for the one made of stone. He will accomplish artistic workmanship in us. If you're reading this and not feeling like a work of art, hang on. He's just not finished yet.

STRATEGIES

You have power to enhance your neural pathways and improve physical health. Try these strategies.

GIVE THANKS

Tell God what you're thinking about all of this, so far. Ask Him to show you more, and to help you apply what you discover. You may not understand it all yet, but be thankful for this and other insight you receive.

CONSIDER YOUR THOUGHTS

Not only do your thoughts set your mental tone, but they also help orchestrate the chemistry and functions of your brain. And, as we now know, thoughts even help form brain structure with links to neural patterns, and myelination. There is much more to come on the subject of our thoughts, and several practical strategies to help with them.

Use scriptures to affirm God's goodness, power and love, and our safety within His care. Make it a practice to find and memorize one such verse every day. Write it in your journal. When negative thoughts swarm, say "Stop," and then read or recite your God-given positive scripture. Keep holding on. If one-a-day seems too much, tackle one per week, and repeat it daily.

STAY POSITIVE

Occupy your mind with challenging ideas, learning, and/or meditation. Read scripture. Connect with another believer for conversation, coffee, or tacos. Learn a musical instrument. Try a new recipe, a hobby/craft or challenging sport. Read a good book or take a class. Add your own inspiration. Aim for some variety. Get busy to keep those neural pathways clear, and healthy.

PUT YOUR BODY IN MOTION

Get your body involved. If you have ever been stuck in a "worry loop," you know how difficult it can be to break free. But, in his book *Worry: Controlling and Using it Wisely,* Dr. Edward Hallowell suggests that if you will get up - and begin to sway, or use any other kind of rhythmic, repetitive movement, at the first sign of worry, you can break free of it.

We can move our emotions by moving our bodies.

Shall we dance? Learning new steps can be a great activity. In fact, any activity that offers a mental challenge, and body movement, can be amazingly effective to lift a bit of the weight of depression. If you don't have a partner for activity, go solo. You can rock or sway, in time with music. Now, try it with your hands raised. Clap to the rhythm, wave your hands or try conducting the music.

GET SOCIAL

When you sense a downward spiral, and temptation calls you to hide in your bed or cover your head, force yourself to get up and get out, even if it seems like a test of endurance. Do one simple thing that requires a change of scene and, if you can, add some kind of social contact.

For example, you could try going out for coffee and speaking to just one human being, like the Barista. If coffee is not your "cup of tea," find some other simple, single thing you can handle. Do it! When you do, be sure to record your success in your journal. You acted even when you didn't feel like it. That proves you can have some control, even when you *feel* helpless.

We need to keep those pathways of inner space well traveled. It's worth the effort. You might surprise yourself and discover new kinds of fun too. Juggling anyone?

SCRIPTURE FOR MEDITATION

"Finally brethren, whatever things are true whatever things are noble, whatever things are just, whatever things are pure, whatever things are lovely, whatever things are of good report; if there is any virtue and if there is anything praise worthy meditate on these things." Philippians 4:8

Chapter 5 — The Fingerprints of God

In addition to the trinity of body, mind, and spirit, brain structure itself is often presented as a product of triune development. While the description and explanation of the brain's structures and function have been organized in a variety of ways, three-part categorization, labeling, and analysis is a standard model.

Depending on what biology texts you've read, stages of brain development may have been labeled as (1) reptilian, (2) mammalian, and (3) the human brain. Those labels align with the three-stage theory of Darwinian evolution, which the Bible rejects. But, if we change the labels to reflect our belief in God's truth of creation, a three-stage description works just fine. We are blessed with three levels of brain function. There is a trinity. It shows in the Maker's mark, the fingerprints of God.

A PRACTICAL DESIGN

Our Creator is as practical as He is amazing. God is free to use any and all parts of His creations in any manner He chooses. He created all life on planet earth—as well as the planet itself, and the universe it spins in. Why couldn't He choose to use variations and parts of His design to accomplish similar basic tasks in different life forms?

Evolutionists claim that since lower life forms have structures to support lower, limited brain function (Levels One and Two), then evolution must be responsible for our higher development too. They propose, it must have continued with the *human* brain's ultimate development to Level three. There are some major, and critical points missing in this proposal. We need to understand the difference between microevolution ("use-it-or-lose-it"), which we see in our everyday lives, and macroevolution (one species evolving into another), which we do *not* see.

It is beyond the scope and the goal of this book to enter the creation vs. evolution debate. Several great texts go into these subjects if you want to read more about them. One resource I can recommend is: *I Don't Have Enough Faith To Be An Atheist* by Norman L. Geisler and Frank Turek.

The best, original, Genesis report proclaims there is nothing accidental in our design: "Then God said, *'Let Us make man in Our image, according to Our likeness; let them have dominion over the fish of the sea, over the birds of the air, and over the cattle, over all the earth and over every creeping thing that creeps on the earth.'* So God created man in His own image; in the image of God He created him; male and female He created them." Genesis 1:26-27

CRUISING: A THREE-SPEED MODEL

We do have a three-speed transmission for cruising inner space. The brain stem is our most basic brain structure. Consider it as Level One (or first gear). This is all about the mechanics of survival.

The Limbic system, at Level Two, is a big step-up in intelligence and development, which processes emotion, and is the seat of memory. It includes the hippocampus, amygdala, hypothalamus, and olfactory areas of the brain.

Level Three brings us to the neo-cortex, the outermost part of the brain's structure. The cerebral cortex hosts our highest conscious functions. It is the home of rational thought, creativity, logic, and learning.

INDIVISIBLE AND INTERACTIVE

It's important to understand this tri-level anatomical structure and organization. While each level operates differently within the limitations of that part of the structure, it's an indivisible, interactive system. Each part affects the whole. We need to be aware of how our thinking, our choices, and experiences affect brain operation.

All three levels of brain operations influence mood, including depression and anxiety, as well as the opposite emotions of joy and peace.

In many surprising ways, we have a role in determining the level of brain function we live with, moment-by-moment. We can learn to use our power to great effect, switching levels either by automatic or manual control. We are in the driver's seat more often than we might realize. It's a God-given privilege, and responsibility, built-in to our divine design.

AUTOMATIC, OR MANUAL CRUISE CONTROL?

We have a switching mechanism that controls which level is in operation at any given moment. This mechanism is called the Reticular Activating System (RAS). The RAS sits at the upper brain stem, and goes upward into the lower parts of the cerebral cortex. It runs on the same fiber wiring we discussed earlier (neurons, axons, and dendrites) and operation depends on the same chemical flows (transmission fluid) at the synapse and throughout the body. All sensory information, (except smell,) is processed by the RAS. It also regulates our wake/sleep cycle transitions.

When we're emotionally charged up, as in the "fight-flight-freeze" response, we're driving on automatic, at Level One. In this gear, the RAS turns off the cerebral cortex (logic, learning, and memory) and many other important functions, redirecting all resources to the immediate needs of survival. Even our immune systems and digestion are turned off.

After all, if we faced such a thing, we would need fast reactions to dodge a semi-truck coming at us with no brakes. There would be no time to learn about, or to compute facts of speed vs. distance. Without stopping to think about it we would *move!* Our instinct, or intensive training would take over, because Level One (survival) is in control.

When the danger is gone our emotions calm down. Once we feel safe again, and we relax, we can shift into a higher gear. Our bodies resume regular functions. Digestion and Immune systems start to work again. Have you ever been ill following a prolonged, stressful period? This is one reason for increased vulnerability.

When the crisis is over and calm is restored, the cerebral cortex (Level Three) can come back on-line. Then we are free to think logically or creatively. We can learn, remember, communicate and make decisions again.

Our interpretation of emotions, sensations of threat or safety, and pleasure or pain, (real, remembered or imagined), dictate the activity at Level Two. This is critical territory. It's the "seat of memory" and the source of much of the good things in life. We shift back and forth between levels of brain function as we go through our days.

While much of this work goes on automatically, without awareness, we have some power over our conditions and responses. We don't always recognize it. The more we do, the better able we are to choose which level of brain function we want to cruise with, shifting gears to meet the changing demands of our day-to-day experience. If we feel stuck in the wrong gear, prayer works better than the most superior transmission fluid imaginable. Meditation can do wonders for re-setting our idle speed and smoothing our transitions.

A switch is a small thing—but has great potential power. In their explanations and discourse, Bible writers used analogies that were familiar to people in their times. They did not have automobiles but they did have ships. Here is an example of the power in small things: "Look also at ships: although they are so large and are driven by fierce winds, they are turned by a very small rudder wherever the pilot desires." James 3:4

Our Pilot is the best. He's the Lord of all of creation. As part of His crew, He allows our hands on the rudder (switch). We need to follow our Pilot's direction. We can learn to use the equipment skillfully.

I hope these 'mechanical' metaphors and analogies simplify and illustrate some of the concepts and operations of inner space. The more we know, the better we will be able to appreciate God's incredible designs, and our privilege to learn navigation and driving skills. We want to make the most of, and enjoy the journeys of our lifetimes.

This is what God wants for us too. He said: *"The thief does not come, except to steal, kill and destroy. I have come that they may have life and that they may have it more abundantly."* John 10:10

Next, we'll take an even closer look at our own ability to impact the workings of our magnificent systems. We will learn much more about the RAS, and how we can intentionally put this powerful system to use—taking us far beyond the ability to survive, helping us to thrive. As we expand, or refresh, our understanding of brain structure and operation, we can put brain-based strategies to work. We can learn to assist the switch.

STRATEGIES

Many people go through life in a semi-conscious state. If we want to live life fully as God wants us to do, then we must notice and add intention as we shift from one gear to the other. Here are some things we can do.

KEEP IT SIMPLE

We are created in God's image. We may not fully understand the depth of meaning in that statement, but we do know that God is revealed to us in the trinity of Father, Son, and Holy Spirit.

God gave us easily understood, and beautiful, simplified examples of Trinity in nature. For example, water is two parts hydrogen and one part oxygen (three elements in one). Water may be expressed as liquid, solid (ice), or vapor (steam), three very different forms, each still fully the same substance. We are created as beings with body, mind/soul, and spirit. This triune example is one way we are created in His image. There may be other ways as well, more wonderful than we can imagine. Why should we be surprised that we can't fully comprehend the *infinite* with our finite minds?

As infinite and complex as He is, we are invited to enjoy child-like simplicity when we pray. "Our Father ..."

CONTINUE TO JOURNAL YOUR UNIQUE STORY

Write the points you found most interesting or most important.

Why did those points resonate with you? Write any unanswered questions. Save space for writing answers as you discover them.

TRACK YOUR EMOTIONAL STATE

Keep monitoring your stress levels. Shift gears as needed by practicing strategies to soothe and reduce tension. Do something—and give yourself credit in your journal. Write down your favorite simple activities. They may inspire you to repeat them.

SCRIPTURES FOR MEDITATION

"For who knows a person's thoughts except their own spirit within them? In the same way, no one knows the thoughts of God except the Spirit of God. What we have received is not the spirit of the world, but the Spirit who is from God, so that we may understand what God has freely given us." 1 Corinthians 2: 11-12

God knows and fully understands our hearts, and all of our thoughts, even when we are confused. When we can't trust our own hearts or may not know what to pray, we have no need to fear. We can ask the Holy Spirit to pray for us.

"Likewise the Spirit also helps in our weakness. For we do not know what we should pray for as we ought, but the Spirit Himself makes intercession for us with groanings which cannot be uttered." Romans 8:26

Blessings!

CHAPTER 6 — RUSH HOUR TRAFFIC

C ongratulations! We've come a long way through inner space, and we've made good time. We will take a short rest, but our journey is far from over. We have glimpsed the structure, operations, and the incredible integration of body, brain, and mind in one connected, dynamic and interactive system.

We've considered the three levels of brain function and structure. We learned that we can choose to shift control from lower levels of survival (Level One), to higher levels of thought, 'connection,' and creativity (Level Three). Our divine design does not restrict us to the limits of 'autopilot'.

Levels of function and brain structures are often referred to separately, but there is no real separation between them. Not only are all levels structurally connected, but also our 'electrical wiring' and our chemistry run through every level, and every system. The neural network covers all of the territories of inner space. It is an integrated system, and it handles two-way traffic (mind-to-body-to-mind) flowing from lower to higher levels, and from right to left-brain hemispheres, from front to back.

We marvel at the speed and direction of the signals. Our brains/minds direct our bodies, and our bodies affect our brains. It's definitely a two-way traffic flow, with multiple lanes. In inner space it's almost always rush hour.

Toes to nose, crown to core, our own personal information highways could make the most advanced, busiest and most futuristic freeway systems seem like barely recognizable, unpaved hiking trails in comparison. Imagine the challenge of traffic control!

We need a clear understanding of our built- in Traffic Control System, because it is another place of powerful opportunity. We can choose to make improvements in our lives, when we learn how to use it.

We can agree with what Psalm 139:1-4 says: "I will praise You, for I am fearfully and wonderfully made; Marvelous are Your works, and that my soul knows very well." Psalm 139:1-4

Our on-ramp is just ahead. The journey continues…

AMAZING BRAINS AT WORK

Our amazing brains work hard to make sense of our world and our experiences. With billions of neurons, and the input from billions more chemical connections constantly sending and receiving information from every part of our bodies, the amount of incoming data would overwhelm us if we had to consciously recognize each bit. Much of that is handled for us by the same Reticular Activating System (RAS), we just explored. This un-glamorous structure is dazzling. It works as our Level Control Switch and as our traffic metering light system.

The RAS works with parts of the Limbic system to keep the rhythms of our sleep-wake cycles, and to manage the estimated 100 million impulses that reach our brains per second. The RAS filters all information and only lets the most essential, unique and/or dangerous information through to our awareness in the cortex. So, how is the sorting accomplished, and by what standards are messages graded?

THE SORT AND SIGNAL SYSTEM

Our survival and safety are a priority. The RAS will trigger awareness when presented with the sights, sounds, smells, or feelings of danger. We will also be alerted to unknown or novel stimuli if it has not, already, been identified as safe to ignore. That's why the unfamiliar creaks and noises in a new home may keep you awake—until you become used to them. Then, you rarely hear them at all.

It is much more than just an alarm. The RAS filter also looks for information that we identify as essential. Our signaling systems operate with a type of minimum current requirement, or 'response threshold'. Neurons won't even react to a stimulus if its signal is too weak to cross our threshold. Without a responsive signal being fired, our cortex (at Level Three) won't get the message at all. It will have been filtered out at lower levels.

Here comes the real excitement. We get to set our own definition of "essential" and we set our own threshold levels. We do this with our attention, our emotions, and our learned behaviors. Our emotions and memories are processed and stored at Level Two.

It's important to remember that assessment and interpretation of emotions, learning of behaviors, recognizing desires, making decisions, and setting goals or making plans are all higher-level activities. They are accomplished at Level Three. If something doesn't get through the filters at Level Two to trigger the response threshold, we may never become aware of it. We may miss the chance for any of those higher-level activities.

Our focus of attention, our expectations, and our emotions are deciding factors in setting thresholds. For example, if we're on the alert for our baby's cry, we'll be aware of the slightest whimper, and not even hear the usual, possibly louder, traffic noise on the street. Sounds of the baby we love and want to care for are highly important to us. The traffic is not significant unless we hear the sudden sound of brakes squealing or a crash nearby.

We can use this understanding to target the things we want to notice or feel and to help reduce physical and/or emotional pains that don't aid us in our journey. We can train our minds and set our own thresholds of attention.

What we decide is important in our lives (what we're focused on), is what we become *capable* of noticing. Those signals will get through our filters. Whatever we do *not* recognize, and tag as important, may not even be able to get our attention.

For me, this adds another layer of meaning to… "seek and you shall find." What are you actively or unconsciously seeking? What do you want to notice in your life? What are you focused on?

AVOID THE BLAME GAME

This information is a source of hope, not blame. My emphasis on how our own free will can impact many levels of brain function does not mean that you cause all of your difficulty. What it does say is that you have some power over your perceptions and responses.

We live in a fallen world, and in fragile human bodies. Historical, environmental, physical, chemical, and spiritual effects can cause trouble every day.

In spite of physical or mental illness, in spite of circumstances, in spite of attack, we can, by the grace of God, still hold on to hope. We can pray. We can discover, and apply the gifts God has designed within us. We can learn and practice strategies to make the most of those gifts, and know that there are biological reasons those strategies work. With the guidance of the Holy Spirit, we can use our awareness, intention, focus and skill-building efforts, to achieve more than we may have imagined.

GOD'S ELEGANT SYSTEM

Neuro-anatomy and physiology study the most elegantly complex system imaginable. It's ours. Our actions, thoughts, beliefs, and expectations impact every part of it, yet we may have spent a lot of our lives not fully knowing the wonderful design we share, and being unaware of our power to affect it.

The Spirit gives life and, at our request (as we tune-in), will guide the choices we make, which drive our whole amazing system. Mind, body, and spirit form the human trinity of life. There are no artificial barriers in our integrated triune systems. We often seem to run on autopilot without recognizing or appreciating this divine interplay.

My heart's desire is that understanding more about God's incredible design will encourage you. It is amazing to learn how it functions, and the abilities He has given us to partner with Him in putting it to work.

STRATEGIES

Knowing God's architecture is one thing, putting it to work another. Here are some ways that can help put your knowledge into action.

PRAYER

Thank God for the miracle of His creation and ask Him to show you who you are, in Christ, and to help you recognize and make the most of His gifts.

JOURNAL HOW SCRIPTURE DEFINES YOU

Write down at least one new gospel verse each week that tells who you are in Christ, and what He says about your value to Him. Tape it up where you will see it every morning (perhaps the bathroom mirror). Read it out aloud before leaving your room, every day. Try memorizing the passages. You are setting your attention. This exercise helps to clear and mend your mental filters.

AFFIRM GOD-GIVEN GOODNESS

Identify three positive things about yourself, your associates, or your circumstances that you would like to see more of. Set yourself a task of noticing whenever one shows up in your day. Do this every day for one week. Then, set three new targets for the same kind of attention. See if you can find at least a 'seed' of one of your targets even in the midst of trouble. This re-sets your filters and "minimum response thresholds" so your brain will notice what you are seeking.

COUNT BLESSINGS, NOT SHEEP

Write down what you have noticed about your seeds before going to bed. Is it getting easier to spot them? Thank God! You are re-programming, and strengthening your ability to notice the good stuff in your life. That will increase your ability to enjoy them, and to reduce the negatives weighing you down.

SCRIPTURE FOR MEDITATION

Proverbs 23:7 says: "As a man thinks in his heart, he is…"

What we have learned puts that verse in a whole new light. There is much more to come.

CHAPTER 7—MISSION CONTROL

Computers and machines can't grow new parts, make new connections or re-wire, and re-program themselves. Our brains can.

ORGANIZATION AND PROCESSING

Each of us is a unique creation, with different life experiences. In response, we may have some slight differences in brain organization and wiring.

Healthy brains operate with a left and a right hemisphere, working together in different ways. These differences have been described as similar to operations of linear and parallel processing units. I am not reducing our magnificent brains to the equal of a machine or computer. Those analogies can offer just a pale suggestion of what our divine designer has actually blessed us with.

Most of us are wired with the left hemisphere of the brain designated as the major site for logic, language, and communication (speech and auditory processing). The left breaks things down and puts them in sequential order, with precise analysis, to construct meaning.

The right hemisphere is most often described as more holistic—with parallel processing of entire experiences (gestalt) of music, art, and spatial concepts.

A simplified illustration may be drawn by looking at differences between an efficient business memo, with sequential bullets highlighting key points of the message—as compared to free poetry, which conveys the images, rhythms, and *feelings* of experience. The logical left hemisphere processes the memo with crisp linear efficiency, while the holistic right expresses poetry-art without itemization or ordered analysis. This reflects two distinctly different processing styles. We need both.

The two sides of our brains work in tandem. Their signals cross the corpus callosum, a bridge of nerve fibers, connecting left and right hemispheres of the brain. The incredible amount and speed of communication between hemispheres are made possible by this structure.

Our systems are cross-wired. Thousands of miles of cross-wired neural connections, through our entire bodies, are key to an incredible division of labor between the left and right hemispheres of the brain.

The left side of the brain controls muscles on the right side of the body and vice-versa. This basic of design supports much greater complexities that enable dazzling performances of movement, balance, coordination, and much more in the business of living.

We can localize sound, in part, because of split-second differences in timing of sound signals from left and right ears, and because of the integration of signals from other parts of the brain. Vision also depends on contra-lateral (cross-wired) connections, and complicated processing patterns which give us depth perception, among other things.

Our cross-wired design also gives us creative adaptability. It is not unusual for a person injured in the left hemisphere (by stroke, trauma or other brain issues), to have great difficulty with speech, yet be able to sing lyrics with ease. We've seen performers who had other speech difficulties, like stuttering, who became famous recording artists. Cross-wired adaptability holds great promise for recovery from other varied injuries too.

Brain space is well organized, with major work areas assigned to specific primary tasks..

EXECUTIVE FUNCTION

Executive Function describes our ability to pay attention, to reflect on, and to hold information in working memory. It allows us to see things from more than one perspective. It enables us to organize and plan, start new tasks, ignore distractions and inhibit behaviors. It helps us to self-monitor and to assess our performance and our wellbeing. Importantly, it empowers us to regulate our emotions. These (Level Three) tasks are assigned primarily to the frontal lobe—the Boss.

MOVEMENT, TOUCH AND FEELING

Motor and Sensory strips are side-by-side, just behind the frontal lobe. Draped over the crown of the head, they reach both left and right sides of the brain. The primary task for the motor strip is to initiate or control voluntary muscle movements. There is much more to the story. Varied parts of the brain work together to accomplish controlled and coordinated fine and gross motor movements. The sensory strip recognizes and controls our senses. Sensations are not necessarily interpreted and given meaning in this single location, but it is key to reception and recognition of sensory signals.

VISION

The eyes are described as the windows of the soul. We receive light information through the eyes, but these signals travel a complex and cross-wired pattern before being processed and interpreted in the Occipital lobe at the back of the brain.

COORDINATION

The Cerebellum (at the lower, back of the brain) receives and integrates information from sensory systems, the spinal cord, and other parts of the brain to fine-tune activity. This is headquarters for coordination, precision, and timing. The Cerebellum predicts movement trajectories, working to prevent over-shooting or under-shooting of targets.

We used to think the Cerebellum's work with coordination was all about motor activity, but newer research (C.L. Highnen and K.M. Belize, 2011) suggested that it works in similar ways on language performance by predicting linguistic outcomes, and error-checking before we express our thoughts in speech. This is another amazing example of integration. No worksite functions in isolation. Constant communication and collaboration are required.

INTEGRATION: THE POWER OF TEAMWORK

To this point, we focused on organization and function of discreet areas of the brain, and offered strategies fit to each part. Even more power is available with teamwork. We access this by engaging multiple areas (work sites) and systems, to work together on the same challenge. Never settle for isolated effort, if you can find some way to add multi-sensory resources.

Imagine a conference table in my classroom, with a paper cup full of water sitting at the center. I asked if a volunteer could come up and lift the table without spilling the water. The rules dictated the table had to be lifted at least six inches off the floor, and the lifter could only use one hand. I had no volunteers. Next, I asked for six volunteers to take positions around the table, two on each side of the rectangle and one at each end. One patient spoke a countdown, to assure everyone would lift together. Using one hand each, they had no problem completing the task, exceeding the six-inch lift, without spilling the water. The table lift illustrated the success we can enjoy with integration and coordination of activity.

There is <u>no</u> absolute separation into isolated job sites within the brain. A physical or mental challenge like learning something new, solving a problem or just taking care of old business calls for teamwork. The work will be easier, faster, more successful, and longer lasting if we get multiple areas involved. The more we can integrate and enlist activity from varied parts of the brain, the better.

You will be glad we took some time here, to explore the organization of brain-works. There are dramatic stories of how our amazing brains can recover from injuries or imbalances, because of this organization of our divine design.

With a basic understanding of our system operations and organization, we can more fully appreciate the intricate architecture of inner space, and our information highways. Traffic is constant, with millions of signals filtered or processed each second, of every minute, of every day.

It's not hard to understand that such a busy, delicate, and carefully balanced system of electrical, chemical, and physical links, could be disrupted by illness, injury, and other factors. We can also be encouraged as we appreciate the rich, incredibly powerful, flexible and amazing design we have been blessed with.

Life may be hard, but it's also filled with promise. We have 'back-up' systems, repair strategies, and potential resilience built-in. These are real, and excellent, reasons for hope.

STRATEGIES

We are not computers. We are, wonderfully, created by God. Computer scientists borrowed their ideas from Him. Computers don't need to connect to God, but humans require it. These strategies help to develop that connection and engage teamwork.

FOCUS ON GOD'S DESIGN

Let God know what you think of His design, and ask Him to help with your understanding and ability to use it fully and wisely.

ACTIVATE YOUR SENSES

Turn a simple walk into a whole brain activity by deliberately noticing what you see, hear, smell, and feel. Amplify it by keeping a specific rhythm. Dance. Bounce a ball as you walk. Sing, or carry on a conversation with a walking buddy. You could carefully try walking backwards for a few steps (to exercise balance). To engage the whole brain in your activity, do things that physically cross the mid-line of your body—right to left, front and back, top and bottom. Use as many senses as you can.

CHALLENGE YOURSELF WITH SKILLED MOVEMENTS

Ride a bike. Try line dancing or square dance, golf, tennis, basketball or any other sport or activity using movement and skill. The brain loves novelty. Try learning to play a musical instrument, or try learning to listen/learn/read/write/speak a new language. How about learning to juggle scarves or balls? This has been especially helpful for those with dyslexia or other learning difficulties, as well as for those in recovery from stroke or traumatic brain injury.

JOURNAL YOUR EXPERIENCES

Keep a record of your activity and your progress in your journal. Give thanks!

SCRIPTURE FOR MEDITATION

"O Lord, how manifold are Your works! In wisdom You have made them all." Psalms 104: 24

CHAPTER 8—BACK-UP: REASONS FOR HOPE

When I was still in graduate school (more than 30 some years ago), the latest rehabilitation science informed us that humans were born with all the brain cells we would ever have, and that our brains were pretty much hardwired by the time we entered adulthood.

For folks who had suffered any brain injury (Traumatic Brain Injuries, Stroke, etc.), therapists-in-training were advised that recovery was limited to whatever gains were made as the brain healed from initial organic damage and swelling. "Best Practice" demanded that we focus therapy on making the best of what was left, and helping our patients to develop alternative methods for difficult activities like re-learning to tie a shoe or to find, or learn to use assistive devices.

We were to focus on habilitation (learning to live with it) rather than re-habilitation (improvement). Thank God, we were completely wrong! We now find that our brains generate new brain cells every day, and that can continue for as long as we live.

These baby brain cells, born in the area of the Hippocampus, need to be nurtured, protected, and given meaningful assignments if they are to survive and grow. Excess stress, and inactivity are brain cell killers.

CARE OF BABY BRAIN CELLS

There are five daily minimum requirements for baby brain cells. The first four include a healthy diet, adequate sleep, stress management, and protection from injury. These are needed for the new cells to thrive and go to work on our behalf.

Meaningful engagement is the fifth requirement. The new cells need a reason for living. We won't engage these new recruits if we do nothing to challenge the brain. Lack of purpose causes them to be discarded. This is another example of our use-it-or-lose-it design. The process of generating new brain cells is called Neurogenesis. It's a beautiful and powerful part of our back-up systems, and a great reason for hope.

BACK-UP SYSTEMS

"Call for back-up" is a familiar line from TV crime drama entertainment, and we enjoy the sentiment in other contexts too. If a friend says, "I've got your back," those are beautiful words. Of course, we computer users cherish our back-up files.

Great news—we have live "back-up", right here in inner space. We don't even have to make a call or hit a "save" button because it's part of our design. Our brain structure, wiring schematic, network operations, and organization all reflect the care and complexity of our design, as does our elegant neural cross-wiring that allows coordination of movement, and sensation.

We're designed with an infinitely complex and delicate system that requires integration for optimal performance. Fine and large motor control, as well as focal and peripheral vision, and depth perception, all work well because of our brain's intricate patterns of network connections. For example, we keep our balance because of cross-wired, full integration of signals coordinating vision, hearing, vestibular function, and muscle control.

Much of this work is done for us, without our awareness or intention. We can also learn to apply *deliberate* efforts, using the effects of integration to strengthen our physical, thinking and learning abilities—including the ability to balance some emotional states.

Disruption of the joint operations of our beautifully delicate system, caused by illness or injury, may be seen as disintegration. We would pay a high price for those disruptions if they were permanent.

Thank God, they often are not. We are blessed with repair and replacement possibilities. We can learn to consciously assist them.

STRATEGIES

Our brain handles most routine things in passive mode. However, we can consciously intervene when we need to do so. Part of the synchronization process is keeping God in the loop. We can choose to include or to exclude Him, but we only become whole when He is at the center of our brainwave activity.

GOD TALK

I define prayer as a conversation between two who love each other—that's you, and God. Talk things over with Him. Tell Him what's on your mind. He knows our every anxious thought, whether we voluntarily share them or not, so why not talk it out? Thank Him for the ways we are fearfully and wonderfully made. Ask Him to show you how to use this information in your moment of need.

KEEP YOUR BRAIN REFRESHED

Get some quality sleep. Begin by turning off the distractions and getting to bed a bit earlier. Establish a bedtime routine. Try deep breathing, meditation and/or other strategies that we will discuss in future chapters to ease your way.

FOCUS ON NUTRITION

Pay attention to what you are feeding your body. Make it the good stuff. Choose nutritious food that benefits your health and avoid the choices you know are bad for your health.

EXERCISE YOUR BRAIN

Think new thoughts. We don't have to focus on repeating the stories of our painful yesterdays. We wear ourselves out with those. Instead, consider that every morning, we have the potential to activate and salvage some of those new brain cells with a positive challenge. Be encouraged.

Take Philippians 4:8 as a challenge. Fill in the blanks about your personal situation and write them in your journal. Do this review regularly and ask: "Does anything in your world qualify for one of these slots?" Put your magnificent brain cells to work searching them out. Date your reviews.

Whatever things are lovely, true, or noble (about _____)

_____;

Whatever things are just (fair, equally valued) about _____

_____;

Whatever things are pure (about _____)

_____;

Whatever things are of good report (about _____)

_____;

If there is any virtue (about _____)—list it here

_____;

If there is anything praiseworthy (about _____)—identify it

_____;

Meditate on these things.

Do this review about specific issues. If a particular problem, person or circumstance is on your mind, insert that *name* as you consider each line. Ask God to help you think creatively. How might you confirm, celebrate and apply the positive truths you discover?

SCRIPTURE FOR MEDITATION

Aging, fatigued or damaged brain cells do not, as once thought, doom us. Instead, we can celebrate new connections, and new baby brain cells, every day. Neuro-genesis and our ability to make new connections are part of God's creative design for us. Think about how these verses may apply.

"Through the Lord's mercies we are not consumed, because His compassions fail not. They are *new every morning;* Great is Your faithfulness." Lamentations 3:22-23

"Behold, I will do a new thing. Now it shall spring forth; shall you not know it? I will even make a road in the wilderness and rivers in the desert." Isaiah 43:19

CHAPTER 9 — MORE HOPE: BACK-UP REVISITED

Ready for more of an introduction to our back-ups? Okay, drumroll please… Ladies and Gentlemen, here before you (and within you) the amazing concept of neuroplasticity.

So what is neuroplasticity, and why should we be excited about it? It's the second component in our back-up system and a lead vehicle to drive healing within the brain. The reference to "plastic" is made, because the brain is so much more moldable than we expected. We can shape patterns of connection to achieve changes in the way the brain works. Change is also possible in the structure itself. The brain can change as a result of our activity, which includes our mental and physical experience.

The Nobel Prize in Physiology or Medicine was awarded in the year 2000, for work demonstrating that learning causes increased connections among nerve cells. Yes, every time we challenge the brain with new learning, we make new physical connections between brain cells. Neurons constantly communicate, electrically and chemically, with each other and with dendritic connections. They can, and do, form and re-form new connections every moment of every day we live.

I love celebration. I think it should be part of our lives at every opportunity. This is a good one. We can rejoice, praise God, and celebrate His infinite wisdom and great love. He knows our weaknesses. He provides back-up for us and gives us an active role to play in the process. We have a powerful impact on how our systems work. We exert that power every day, even when we're not aware of it, and we can learn to use it to help make our lives easier and more fulfilling.

CREATIVE POSSIBILITIES

We can re-wire, and re-program our brains when we effectively, and deliberately, put neuroplasticity to work. This holds great potential. If one pattern of brain cell connections (formed by mastery and repeated use of a skill or action) is disrupted by illness, injury, or neglect, we can re-program, or re-pattern, by forming new connections. We do this by finding new ways to achieve the desired outcome and then repeating the new methods until they become a new hardwired pattern.

DOIDGE'S INSIGHT

In his fascinating book, *The Brain's Way of Healing*, Dr. Norman Doidge explained that <u>while mental activity is a product of the brain, it also shapes it</u>. For example:

- If neural pathways are lost because of neglect, with no other damage, then connections and patterns for abilities we once had, may be restored and strengthened if we simply re-commit to repeated practice, and invest enough time and effort.

- If function was disrupted by trauma or injury to brain cells, it is possible to form new connections, and new patterns of connection (neural pathways) with other brain cells in that same sector. We do that by learning new ways to accomplish things. New routes, or circuits, within the neural network can be established to by-pass damaged areas.

Learning new ways to walk, talk, or move, after an injury, takes more time, intention, and repetition because we are building new circuitry. Think of the networked patterns that have wired together, as a type of work site. If we need to expand, re-route or build new sites, our work may be slowed or become more difficult during construction.

IT'S MORE THAN A THEORY

In recovery classes at Napa State Hospital, I asked my patients to imagine being given a golden ticket to a great event in San Francisco, like the World Series, or Super Bowl. I asked if they could get to the game if the Bay Bridge was shut down. Of course, they thought of an alternative, like using Highway 37 to 101 and then crossing the Golden Gate Bridge.

I went on asking, "What if… the Golden Gate was also out of order and the Dumbarton Bridge was closed? What if the Vallejo Ferry was shut down and the Sausalito/Marin Ferry was closed." They finally decided that they could drive south to circle the bay at San Jose, and then come back up the peninsula to San Francisco. Of course, if that golden ticket included a good-sized cash award, they would charter a helicopter or boat of their own.

We had a few good laughs with this exercise. The point was that even with many different areas of damage or difficulty they would be able to find an alternate route, to get *close* to their target. They just had to be willing to go the extra miles, and put in repeated effort. Alternate routes certainly would not be as fast, convenient, smooth, or easy as the tried-and-true routines they were accustomed to, but the potential for eventual success was real.

The same possibilities exist in inner space. We can find alternate neural pathways (routes) to approach our goals with brain function, even if we need to detour some areas.

But, what if the damage, or trauma caused too many casualties in a specific area? Or, what if communication was disrupted so we couldn't call rookies, the new brain cells, or our regular back-up players into the game? Well then, in addition to building detours, we may need to recruit brain cells from different sectors to do the job of those that have been lost. The amazing thing is, we can do that.

LOCATION, LOCATION, LOCATION

A real estate agent would view the San Francisco Bay Area as a hot and highly competitive market. Undeveloped land with a view is rare. Demand is extremely high. But that's nothing compared to the competitive market of inner space. We are each limited to our own three-pound brain area.

Every perception, sensation, emotion, thought, desire and action operates, in that small territory. What price can be put on that kind of real estate? God's word says that we are precious to Him. If ever you doubt your worth, think of the ultimate price He paid.

Employment resources are also incredibly competitive in inner space. Much needs to be done, with a limited resource of skilled, creative workers, which is the role of our highly specialized brain cells.

NEUROPLASTICITY IS A GIFT

We've already established that our designer God doesn't waste a thing. He is as practical as He is amazing. So, if we have brain cells primarily assigned to a specific job, but because of inaction, communication breakdown, or damage to job sites (neural pathways and connective ability) they are unemployed, then other work sites may expand into that idle territory. They recruit cells by sending out connectors via a new route for different work.

These work transfers and new connections happen in the usual way, by paying attention, engaging in *targeted* active challenge, repeating the efforts, and then repeat, and repeat, and repeat again, until new ways of taking care of business are established. Once the transfers are made, recruited cells serve different functions and are connected to different job sites within the brain.

Worksite relocation in the brain (communication via alternate pathways) is neuroplasticity in action. What brain functions might be retrained after accident or injury, illness, or neglect? Since we don't know what the limits might be, we can't justify hopelessness.

Paul tells us in Philippians 4:13: "I can do all things through Christ, who strengthens me." May that encourage us. We are in the hands of a mighty God who loves us. He has a heavy investment in our lives and in our joy. We are part of His grand design.

STRATEGIES

You can use the science of neuroplasticity in your own life. It is a matter of consciously routing or re-routing your activity or thought patterns. Here are a few strategies for doing that.

PRAY

Tell God what you think about all that you have read. Ask His help in applying the parts that are important for to you.

MENTAL AND PHYSICAL ACTIVITY

Keep busy with challenging or creative mental or physical activity. Give those potential new baby brain cells, a reason for living. Remember our use-it-or-lose-it design.

CHALLENGE YOUR ROUTINES

If you have always brushed your teeth with your right hand, try it with your left. Could you do it while standing on one leg? How about making your way into the car without looking? Close your eyes or wear a blindfold if it is safe to do so.

These are some of the 83 exercises suggested in a book called 'Neurobics' by: L. Katz, and M. Rubin. Their activities were designed to shake up daily routines by using the five senses in new or different ways, thus creating new neural pathways and stimulating old ones.

Check out the book for yourself, or think up your own ways to do the same old things in new ways. Use as many senses as possible. Perhaps you could use a different route to get to a familiar place, or try identifying a place or thing by sounds or smells you encounter.

WRITE WHAT YOU SEE AND SENSE

What have you noticed lately? Are you still reading and memorizing scripture as you greet your mornings? Are you spotting any blessings in disguise? Does knowing more about your potential for renewal encourage you? I hope so.

The sad/bad/hopeless thoughts of depression may not be as permanently hardwired into our brains as we believed. As we engage in conscious, positive challenges, neurogenesis and neuroplasticity suggest we can re-wire and re-program ourselves. Ask God to give you a new vision. He will add strength, comfort, and help.

SCRIPTURE FOR MEDITATION

"Now to Him who is able to do immeasurably more than all we ask or imagine, according to his power that is at work within us, to Him be glory in the church and in Christ Jesus throughout all generations, for ever and ever!" (Ephesians 3:20) Amen!

CHAPTER 10—SPACE PIRATES AND HEAD HUNTERS

Have you ever heard the term "Head Hunter" used in reference to an employment recruiter? Head Hunters actively seek talented unemployed or under-employed, staff to fill highly specialized, professional positions in business, technology and science.

Pirates are a different kind of Head Hunter. They try to steal talent from competitors to meet existing or increasing demands, with promises of more meaningful or rewarding work. By now, it may not surprise you to know that both headhunting and piracy-types of brain cell recruitment occur in the business of inner space. It's part of our incredible resilience.

Brain injury, stroke or illness may result in loss of abilities, caused by the death or injury of neurons, which leaves them too badly damaged to operate. Damaged cells may survive and continue to attempt communication. But they may lack direction, fire randomly, or send messages that are slower, or out of sync with others in their program. This creates a kind of static in the system—which can affect all other networks.

Clear communication between cells may become much more difficult as a result of this interference. Restless confusion, loss of focus, and frustration are by-products of such noise.

Apart from brain cell injury or death, damage to the area itself, or disrupted lines of communication may also put a worksite out of business. Surviving brain cells might be okay, but if they are stuck in damaged areas, they may be disconnected from the network. Healthy cells can't function if they are cut off from the neural network, because of damage that blocks their signals in or out. Even though they may still be able-bodied cells, they are out of work.

Disruption of healthy brain-works may also be triggered by something like voluntary business closure. If we choose to withdraw from life, allowing prolonged isolation and inactivity (a common risk with depression), we contribute to the under-employment of our precious neurons.

Remember the risks to our neural pathways. Connections weaken and eventually dissolve if they are not used. We risk loss. We can re-engage again if we invest more time and effort to link-up. We must *choose* to do the work. That choice is ours as long as we live.

EMPLOYMENT OPPORTUNITIES

If broken communication is the problem, we can form new links and reconnect. It may take quite a bit of time and exploration, through trial and error (with repeated practice), to find the best route, re-wire and then strengthen new connections, but it can be done. We are never without hope.

How do we know if brain cells in an area are still functional, but disconnected, or if they are no longer operable? And, if we need to form new pathways, how do we know which alternate route will work best?

The short answer is that we *don't* know until we try. We have unknown potential that we must explore. We have a rich inter-connected network, capable of two-way traffic flow, to help us do that.

We do know real estate in inner space is limited. It's a highly competitive market. We can also appreciate how valuable pools of extremely talented, but currently unemployed, brain-cell-specialists are.

Recruiting and putting these specialists to work requires setting up a communication system to the new worksite. We do that by paying attention, engaging in challenges, and repeating the activity over time.

THE PIRATES APPEAR

So, how is piracy involved? Suppose we have staff, working at their regular performance, in a busy and un-damaged site when a different site becomes overwhelmed with a strong, unexpected demand. That flooded work-site will be desperate to find more help. In this case, it's not casualties, or damaged communication that disrupts the flow. More than just noise in the system—there is signal interference and jamming. If demand is high enough, cells can temporarily lose their original orders and are drafted to a new cause.

Think of quiet instructions being overwhelmed by loudspeakers or fire-alarm sirens going off in an emergency. For example, pain signals can over-ride regular activities in the brain. We don't reason, learn, remember or create very well when we're coping with significant pain. Our cells, which were involved in normal function, are now "pirated" in service of transmitting pain messages. This is a safety procedure, and it works very well. Pain is the body's signal that something needs to stop or change, immediately, to avoid further damage.

One risk is that as the message is repeated, those pathways get stronger. Over time, the nerves become increasingly excited and more sensitive and, require less of the original pain signal to fire up the alarms. In such a cases, we can say that piracy is underway for those cells that have been taken from their regular assignments.

Even after the immediate cause of the pain alarm is removed, highly sensitized new transit routines may become much stronger, faster, better insulated, and more continuously used. Thus, we develop a hair trigger on this routine, and get stuck in the loop, at the expense of the normal function that used to work so well. Cells that fire together also *wire* together, and so a new pathway is formed.

Why do we need to know this? It's worth knowing because we can use our understanding of neural recruitment and piracy to change things. We can help restore healthy balance and activity, rather than continuing to be overwhelmed.

Once safety is restored, we can deliberately put emphatic demand on the pirated cells' original programming. As these new demands increase in urgency, driven by our deliberate attention and repeated activity, the signal strength of our original programming can increase enough to cut through the noise and interference.

Our first attempts may be shaky and short-lived, but with repeated, and relentless practice, we can learn to disrupt some of those alarm signals. In doing so, we may be able to reduce the impact of pain, or other overwhelming signals, and re-engage our talented cells in their original work. The pirates can be vanquished.

EVIDENCE OF SUCCESS

Here is an amazing example reported in The Brain's Way of Healing: by Dr. N. Doidge. It's a the story of Michael Moskowitz, M.D., a psychiatrist who became a pain specialist (at Bay Area Medical Associates, Sausalito, California). After exhaustive research into neuroscience, Dr. Moskowitz determined to apply what he learned about neuroplasticity (and piracy) to disrupt his own chronic pain, which resulted from a previously serious, but now healed injury.

He detailed all that was known about major brain areas where his pain was processed, and the original (known) work assigned to those sites. He decided to force those areas to re-engage in their original assignments by flooding them with immediate, and amplified, competing demands every single time that he noticed the start of pain signals.

He identified one pirated brain area as being normally able to process sensory input, such as vibration and touch. He experimented by flooding his body with such sensations, at the first twinge of pain. This forced the area to cope with competing messages, which weakened the demands that piracy had imposed. He noticed some slight improvement.

Next, since visual processing uses a huge amount of brain resources, some of which may have been pirated to send pain signals, he added visualization tasks as another competing activity. He did this every time he noted pain, without exception. This strategy required constant vigilance, determination, and relentless application, but it worked. Within six weeks of using these tactics he reported some reduction in pain, and within a year he was generally pain-free.

Neurons that "fire together—wire together." They form a linked pattern. The pattern can be changed. Neurons that "fire apart—wire apart," making a linked pattern more difficult or impossible to maintain.

This example shows neuroplasticity in action. It's part of the back-up design that our creator included in His master plan. We get to cooperate in our own healing. How great is that?

EXPANDING THE PRINCIPLE

So far, we have focused on the benefits of neuroplasticity relative to healing from a physical injury. But, why couldn't the same principles apply to certain mental distress? If we learn to monitor our mental pain, as well as our physical pain, could we achieve somewhat similar results?

MARGARET LALICH, M.S., M.A.

We can identify emotions or thinking patterns that pirate our wellbeing by overwhelming our peace of mind. Neuroplasticity suggests that we might use competing positive signals to refocus (to weaken the strength of negatives). We can re-frame, or recruit help from outside resources to accomplish this. For example, competing messages of worry and worship cannot equally co-exist in the same space, at the same time. We can use one to loosen the grip of the other. Can't the same be true for mental pain and praise?

Coupling these ideas with the deliberate resetting of our RAS filters to seek "…whatsoever things are lovely" Philippians 4:8, provides a powerful boost to our efforts, and our success, in the battle against depression. This is a valuable recovery skill.

There is an explosion of knowledge that we are just beginning to appreciate in brain science. We truly don't know what all may be possible in the future. We have just started to explore the depths of our reasons for continuing to hope.

Winston Churchill, Britain's Prime Minister during WWII, famously advised that we should, "never, ever give up." That advice was given long before, in the New Testament Gospel. The Apostle Paul said, "And let us not grow weary while doing good, for in due season we shall reap if we do not lose heart." Galatians 6:9

With those assurances, and knowing that we can't set any knowledgeable limits on possibilities for recruitment, regeneration, reprogramming, and recovery—we have more than a license to explore our unknown potentials; we have a *mandate*. We have every reason to be hopeful as we do.

STRATEGIES

Neuroplasticity implies that we can change our thinking patterns. We do not need to be the victim of thoughts that hold us back. The fact that we can change the way we think, and that doing so can improve the function and even the *structure* of our brains, is a wonderful gift from God.

PLEASE & THANK YOU

Give thanks, and talk things over with the lover of your soul. Ask Him to reveal the thoughts that are holding you back. Ask for what you need to grow emotionally and spiritually.

ENGAGE YOUR BRAIN FUNCTIONS

Employees vulnerable to recruitment are those that lack sufficient, meaningful challenge, or the ability to function in their current location. We can keep our brain cells fully engaged in meaningful activity by study, or by taking on challenging physical, or mental, activities which line up with our beliefs and desires.

If a brain area (worksite) is damaged, you may not be able to do the things you used to do, in the same way. Don't give up. Try another way. New links are possible. Remember that physical and mental signals both use the same two-way routes for transmission. Use your body—to assist your mind. Idleness, and isolation are dangerous in inner space.

CHALLENGE NEGATIVE THOUGHT PATTERNS

We can weaken the influence of pirate signals by competing with their transmissions. Worry and worship cannot equally co-exist in the same space, and time. Pessimism and praise are also uneasy mates.

Immediately, at first recognition of painful thoughts, fight back. Compete with the positive power of praise, and amp-up those good signals with added physical sensations such as movement, hearing, sight, and touch, which can be combined. David danced before the Lord—why don't we?

RE-PROGRAM

You must believe it is possible, and make an active choice to become aware of your thoughts. Listen to your self-talk. Catch negatives that cause pain, then check and challenge them.

If your troubling thoughts relate to painful truth accept it, but keep it in perspective, and realize that it's subject to revision. Do what you can to correct or improve the situation, or to balance your responses. Once the cause of the pain is addressed or removed, try the strategies described to combat recruitment and piracy.

KEEP A RECORD OF LOVELY THINGS

Actively seek "whatever things are lovely." Look back in your journal and recognize the good that you have gained. Celebrate each positive step you have recorded in your journal. Realize that your notes are evidence of success (like stones of remembrance). You took steps. You proved that you are not helpless. Every bit of progress or moment of victory proves that hope is not dead. Let that truth sink in. Reaffirm your favorite Bible promise verses. Read them aloud and think of them often, through the days.

SCRIPTURES FOR MEDITATION

Remembering the trials and tribulations Job faced, and considering all that we now know about the science of Neurogenesis and Neuroplasticity (new growth and connections), we can fully appreciate his positive observation:

"For there is hope for a tree, If it is cut down, that it will sprout again, And that its tender shoots will not cease." Job 14:7

We can thank and praise our God for His love and His mercies, as we struggle with our trials. This is a sacrifice of praise. We can also take comfort in the apostle Paul's words:

"For it is the God who commanded light to shine out of darkness, who has shone in our hearts to give the light of the knowledge of the glory of God in the face of Jesus Christ. But we have this treasure in earthen vessels, that the excellence of the power may be of God and not of us. We are hard-pressed on every side, yet not crushed; we are perplexed, but not in despair; persecuted, but not forsaken; struck down, but not destroyed... Therefore we do not lose heart. Even though our outward man is perishing, yet the inward man is being renewed day by day. For our light affliction, which is but for a moment, is working for us a far more exceeding and eternal weight of glory." 2 Corinthians 4: 6-9; 16-17

Earthen vessels are clay pots, which are somewhat fragile in the rough and tumble of every day living. Cracks are not uncommon. I have a few. Congratulations, from one cracked pot to another. Our first exploration of inner space is complete. We'll enter deeper orbit in the next stage. Stay with me.

PART TWO:
MIND MATTERS

The word "psychology" combines the Greek word *psyche*, which means "breath, principle of life, soul," with the term *'logia,'* from the Greek *logos*, which means "speech, word, reason."

When we refer to mind matters, we're talking about psychology. Believers don't need to fear conflict between spiritual and psychological counsel or treatment, even if there has been some confusion in the past. We can seek help from specialists who will honor our beliefs, while using therapeutic approaches familiar to the secular world. We can thank God for both.

Welcome to Part two (Mind Matters). It's all about living with depression because, even in the dark, finding more love, joy, and hope is possible. And it matters.

A Prayer:

May you be blessed, and protected. May you find comfort as understanding grows. May your mind, and heart, be strengthened by our Lord, whose strength is perfected (perfectly displayed) in our weakness. In Jesus' name, Amen.

"Therefore I remind you to stir up the gift of God which is in you. For God has not given us a spirit of fear, but of power and of love and of a sound mind." 2 Timothy 1:6-7

CHAPTER 11—DEPRESSION 101

O ur "Rock of Gibraltar" crumbled on a night when food, fun, and laughter filled a room crowded with family and friends. Joe, who had gone still, suddenly jerked to his feet. He bolted. With tears streaming from slightly panicked eyes, he ran seeking privacy. His sobs echoed through our shock. What just happened? This veteran of two wars—our "Iron Man"—the one who always held the rest of us together, was crying? Where did *that* come from?

Joe had been battling his diagnosed depression for months. But this was something new, unimaginable, and frightening. I chased him down the hall asking questions and offering comfort. I wanted to *fix* this thing. Instead, I added drama to his embarrassment.

I was a great example of what *not* to do.

I finally understood enough to give the poor man a break, and let him be. When the episode passed, and after he caught his breath, he rejoined the family. As calm was restored, Joe even managed to find a type of comic relief from my 'drama'. Laughter can sometimes be found in the midst of tears.

Later, we learned that even with medication, unexpected and uncontrollable crying is one potential symptom of clinical depression. It's not fatal. It will pass. It's just a potential part of the package. Because we didn't know, these events seemed more scary and serious than they needed to. Knowledge is power.

CLEAR DEFINITIONS

Let's agree on what depression is—and what it is not. The Diagnostic and Statistical Manual 5th Edition (DSM-V) sets the standard for the fields of psychiatry and psychology. It does a great job of describing what depression is. It does not examine *why* we are depressed. Seek those answers with individual counsel.

The DSM-V defines depression by listing the criteria for a diagnosis. I have paraphrased them here.

A. Five (or more) of these symptoms during a single 2-week period, which mark a change from previous abilities and conditions including; "…either depressed mood or loss of interest or pleasure."

Symptoms of depression do not include those related to a medical condition, delusions or hallucinations—which are unmatched to mood. Symptoms may be self-reported or observed by others as follows:

- Depressed mood (e.g., feels empty or sad; tearful) most of the day, nearly every day.

- Loss of interest or pleasure in activities, most of the day, nearly every day.

- Weight change of more than five percent per month (plus or minus), not related to dieting, or near daily decreased or increased appetite.

- Sleep imbalance: too much, or too little sleep nearly every day (insomnia or hypersomnia).

- Excessive need to move, or lack of movement, nearly every day (recognized by others). This is more than just feeling restless or being slowed down.

- Fatigue or loss of energy nearly every day.

- Feelings of worthlessness or undeserved guilt, nearly every day. This is more than just regret about being sick.

- Reduced ability to think or concentrate, or make decisions, nearly every day.

- Repeated thoughts of death (not just fear of dying). Thoughts of suicide, a suicide attempt or a specific plan for committing suicide.

B. The symptoms cause significant distress, or reduced social, occupational or other important abilities.

C. The symptoms are not caused by effects of a medical condition, such as hypothyroidism, or use of a substance, like medication or drug abuse.

Praise God, no one experiences every symptom of depression, every day. Each has his/her own unique mix of the five symptoms required for an official diagnosis. But patterns do exist. We classify them by their effects on our biology, psychology, social, and spiritual wellbeing. Symptoms are not fun to look at, but knowing what to expect, helps us prepare with less shock, fear, and pain. Knowledge is power.

WHAT DEPRESSION IS *NOT*

Depression is not a sin, character flaw, a failure of faith, or a sad attention-seeking game. It's not a philosophy, and it's not laziness. It also is not something that we are, and must remain, completely helpless against. Depression does not have to be a mysterious force that keeps us from being who we were created to be, and that is— grateful, capable, and compassionate, children of a loving God. It might just feel that way sometimes.

Physical health, experience, diet, life-style, stress, spirituality, and community all play important parts in maintaining our mental health. We will not be able to fully cover each of these topics in the space of this book, so we'll hit some highlights and include references in the bibliography.

This book does not hold a cure, but it does offer hope. We can cope. Effective, practical, and evidence-based self-help strategies exist. We will explore more than one hundred of them. Let's begin with a most important truth:

YOU ARE NOT ALONE

More than 50 million Americans suffer from full-fledged, diagnosed, mental illnesses such as depression and anxiety, or some other mental/emotional difficulty. Millions more suffer from milder forms that don't meet the criteria for diagnosis but still cause enough pain or chaos to interfere with their lives. No one is immune. It's a no-fault illness that requires treatment as well as faith, and personal effort for recovery.

In years past, we noted depression frequently occurred in adults in their mid-twenties or older. Today, we see widespread depression among 14 year-olds, and recent research shows that approximately 45% percent of college students suffer depression severe enough to impair their cognitive abilities.

About 16 million adults were diagnosed with at least one major depressive episode in the last 12 months. You are not alone if you struggle with this issue.

INTERPRETATION

Some symptoms are described as being "positive" or "negative." This is useful, but it can be confusing if we think in terms of quality instead of quantity. How can symptoms of major depression be a positive (good) thing?

Confusion clears when we think in mathematical terms. Addition is positive (+) and subtraction is negative (-). We can recognize the effects that depression adds to our experience or subtracts from our resources.

This idea offers clues for coping. If a symptom we experience feels like a loss of something, we can work to identify what we need. If one strength or activity is not available, maybe we can find an alternate, or a way to reduce our need.

We have God-given resources and strengths we may not have realized we possess. We need to find these gifts within. We can design self-help tools, and build coping skills, but we need the "specs" to do so. Brain science and newer research offers a peek at the blueprints of our divine design.

GOOD NEWS

Depression is one of the most successfully treated mental illnesses. The key is to get the help we need. A growing variety of medical and non-medical help is available. Medications aren't for everyone, but never mistake use of medication for evidence of character flaws or lack of fortitude.

It is not a sin to use the gifts that our God provides. Most of us have no difficulty with the use of insulin, blood pressure, and other medication for physical relief. I whole-heartedly believe anti-depressive medication can also be taken, if needed, with thanks to God for the knowledge and availability.

Full-blown clinical depression changes the chemistry of the brain. To combat it, we need to disarm chemical weapons. Balance can often be restored naturally, over time, but in the heat of battle we may need more immediate, possibly temporary, firepower. Medication does not seek to change you; it just levels the battlefield by helping to restore balance.

It should not be a Do-It-Yourself project. Work with your doctor. If your doctor is not familiar with medication, diets or supplements you want to consider, get a second opinion, or check with other professionals such as nutritionists, homeopathic doctors, or other therapists.

Please keep an open mind. Medical research, proper nutrition, and the physical ability to participate in exercise, are gifts. Every good gift is from God. Ask Him for guidance. Let's gratefully explore the options to find what works for us, and to seek the help we may need.

TO YOUR HEALTH

Several leaders in functional or holistic medicine, nutrition, and other biological science think that while medication can be life-saving for those who really need it, it is not always the first, best choice for treatment.

Dr. Mark Hyman and others suggest we make good use of the "FARMacy" before turning to the Pharmacy. Dietary changes can make profound differences in our physical and mental health. Exercise can also make a tremendous difference. Studies have shown that exercise can favorably compete with some antidepressant medication. We will examine these topics, in detail, in up-coming chapters.

Treatment is not now, and never will be, a one-size-fits-all project. Each person is unique, so each successful treatment must be custom tailored. Whether balance is achieved through diet, exercise, or medication—it's all good. If medication is needed, use it. If it's not, praise God. Recovery may require more than one approach.

Major depression has a smaller twin, which also creates very real pain and chaos for many who may not qualify for a formal clinical diagnosis. If this describes you, or someone you care for, take heart. Strategies that work for major depression and anxiety disorders are equally effective with the "unofficial" forms of it too. Symptoms are much the same. Differences will be in the numbers of symptoms experienced, and in their intensity, frequency, or duration.

JOE'S STORY: A FINAL NOTE

Joe was as shocked by his sudden outburst of tears as we were, and he was embarrassed to have us see him lose control. We learned that when familiar symptoms popped up, we should quietly let him cope, or offer whatever support he asked for. Coping skills became part of the fabric of our lives. We learned to "roll with it." Life is better when we understand symptoms as threads in the fabric of our life-designs rather than catastrophic unraveling.

A sharp wit and generous spirit were some of Joe's great gifts. He applied them as we journeyed together from tears, to laughter again, and again. We could not find a way to avoid trials, but we did find meaning in them. We were able to trade some of God's promises for our particular pains. We learned the benefits of offering a "sacrifice of praise." We learned to praise God *anyway;* not in thanks for a trial—but most definitely in thanks for getting through it.

Remember the function of the brain's R.A.S., and that worry and worship can't occupy the same mind/mouth at the same time. Praise broke through the tunnel vision of pain, and expanded our focus. We grew stronger and more quickly able to notice, rejoice, enjoy and celebrate the good times.

My dear one also described gaining "Depression Radar" through his trials. He seemed to know who needed encouragement, and to be able to offer the right words, at the right times, for comfort. The only way to gain that kind of skill is to have survived similar experience.

I have his permission to tell this story. Joe wanted to share, if it might be helpful, as this verse suggests:

"Blessed be the God and Father of our Lord Jesus Christ, the Father of mercies and God of all comfort, who comforts us in all our tribulation, that we may be able to comfort those who are in any trouble, with the comfort with which we ourselves are comforted by God." 2 Corinthians 1:3-4

MORE ENCOURAGEMENT

In his book, 'Man's Search for Meaning', Victor Frankl, a survivor of WW II death camps, said we can survive our suffering if we can find meaning in it. I pray this book will help you find meaning, strategies, and comfort.

As the master builder, we know God doesn't waste material. So, we can take even more encouragement in knowing that this pain, this weakness, this trial, and every one of our small victories, will contribute to the beauty and strength of His final design, even if we can't yet see it.

God has great promise for us. While *we* may set the bar so high on our own standards of behavior or achievement that we feel over-whelmed, helpless, or hopeless when we miss the mark, God doesn't.

Psalm 103:13-14 says, "As a father pities his children, so the Lord pities those who fear Him. For, He knows our frame. He remembers that we are dust."

Fear, in this context (for believers), means love and respect. God doesn't depend on us to always walk confidently, and perfectly, to fulfill His plans. Even when our emotions deny it, or when we need medical treatment, counseling or to develop and use coping skills, His truth remains. We are loved. We are not alone. We're invited to "come-as-we-are." We need not fear using any or all of the tools God gives us. Help exists. Hope is real. We need each other to find, and to apply it for our own mutual benefit, and for the glory of God.

CHEERS!

Success doesn't come in isolated cases. It can come in every case, but it doesn't always look the same. We must each define success for ourselves. My triumph might look like a mess to you. We each use our own measure. Today I may need four ounces of goodness and mercy, for my cup to "runneth over." You may need eight, and I might need much more tomorrow. Feelings change. Measure progress one-day-at-a-time.

Operating within God's will, assures eventual victory here or hereafter. God's will is that we know Him and keep His commands. He stated His commands clearly in Mark 12:30-31: *"...And you shall love the Lord your God with all your heart, with all your soul, with all your mind, and with all your strength. This is the first commandment. And the second, like it, is this: You shall love your neighbor as yourself. There is no other commandment greater than these."*

Did you notice the term "yourself" is included in the command to love? This is not selfish, egotistical self-love, setting us above our neighbors, but love to recognize who we are in Christ. We are children of the King. This love does not support mental or physical self-harm. It does not allow devaluation. It clears our hearts of shame, draws us closer to our Lord, and inspires us to be our best selves, in service to others—to the glory of God. The Spirit of God lives within the heart, mind and body of each believer in Christ. Even when we feel completely alone, we are not.

STRATEGIES

We may think life is random, but our lives unfold according to a plan. Here are some strategies that can help you see your life under God's guidance.

FEED ON THE GOOD THINGS

Review your promises from God, and the verses you are committing to memory that tell of His love and of your great worth to Him. Talk things over with Him. Take time in your day to review "whatsoever things are lovely." You are re-programming your brain, resetting your reality, and adjusting your response thresholds to recognize the "good stuff" you don't want to miss.

READING, WRITING AND RECOGNITION

Second only to God, you are becoming the world's greatest expert about you, and that's how it should be. Can you identify something you've learned or achieved? Have you noticed something new? Your observations will pay great dividends.

MAP YOUR SYMPTOMS

Write down, your unique mix of depressive or anxious symptoms in your journal. Learn to spot the moments, hours or days of the week, and the contexts as symptoms appear. Note the frequency and duration. Assign a 5-point rating scale to symptoms as they show up (zero = minimum; five = maximum). Make a note of activities you are using to find relief, and of how well they're working.

Are you using behavioral, dietary or exercise routines? How is it going? Has anything changed? Are you taking medication? Did you miss or delay use? Have they been changed? There are a variety of medications available, and prescriptions are not "one-size-fits-all." Bodies change over time. Adjustments may be needed, in what you're doing, in your frequency or timing. That's why it's called the "practice" of medicine.

This rating will be a guide for you and for your health-care partners as you learn to adjust your meds or coping strategies to meet changing needs. This close study is not just self-indulgence. It's an education. It's valuable. You can do it.

MAP YOUR VICTORIES

Once you have identified symptoms and know what to look for, use a calendar (or journal pages) to rate your day. Be sure to identify at least one thing you are grateful for each day, and thank God.

Give yourself credit for, and write down, any small success you had today. For example, did you get up and do something positive when you felt totally negative? When things felt bad, were you able to identify one 'good' thing, and thank God for it? If so, bravo! These evidences of your success become rocket fuel as you continue your journey to recovery.

There is great power in being able to say of a struggle, "I know I can survive or cope with this because I have done it before." Seriously, don't rob yourself of the evidence of your success. Your

journal review is a power tool for the future. Remember what can easily be lost to memory. Write it down!

SCRIPTURE FOR MEDITATION

"For I know the thoughts that I think toward you, says the Lord, thoughts of peace and not of evil, to give you a future and a hope." Jeremiah 29:11

CHAPTER 12—CARE GIVERS: WHO'S WHO?

A t the end of her day, depressed and tired, Ellie headed for her silent, empty home. She dreaded a lonely struggle through another "long night of the soul," and prayed, "...Lord, I need help. I don't know where to turn or who to trust. Forgive me. I can't do this alone."

Can you relate? I think most of us can. If you were writing this story, what would happen next? What would you share with this character? Should she be surprised or feel guilty about needing more than her our own strength, and faith, to stand against depression, anxiety, or grief and loss? Should we?

Consider that our need for help is well known to our Lord. He said a lot about it, and attached no shame. He delights in our willingness to admit our needs and to accept help. In fact, God acknowledged and addressed our needs for companionship and help right from the beginning. The Lord God said, *"It is not good for the man to be alone. I will make a helper suitable for him."* Genesis 2:18

Our need for each other is often repeated throughout scripture. For example: "Two are better than one, because they have a good return for their labor: If either of them falls down, one can help the other up. But pity anyone who falls and has no one to help them up. Also, if two lie down together, they will keep warm. But how can one keep warm alone? Though one may be overpowered, two can defend themselves. A cord of three strands is not quickly broken." Ecclesiastes 4: 9-12

A cord of three—that's you, and me, and He. United in love, we are strong.

God promised His direct help to those who accepted the invitation to be His people. That promise is equally good today. And, if you have not yet accepted, the offer is still open. Just ask Him.

To believers, He said: *"I took you from the ends of the earth; from its farthest corners I called you. I said, 'You are my servant'; I have chosen you and have not rejected you. So do not fear, for I am with you; do not be dismayed, for I am your God. I will strengthen you and help you; I will uphold you with my righteous right hand."* Isaiah 41:9-10

God hears every prayer, and answers immediately or, on a different schedule, in His time. He may answer with miracles or supernatural intervention. But, He loves to let us share, and often uses His children to serve as His earthly, visible, hands and feet. When we see tragedy or injustice, we may cry out for God to *do something.* The truth is that He already has. He created and empowered us. We are the "somethings" that can make a difference.

REACH OUT

For all of our needs and struggles, prayer is our best, and first line of defense. God is the source of healing and comfort. He often brings people into our lives to deliver His help. We are called to care for each other. We are each uniquely gifted for this service with our own blend of talents, passions, and experiences. If we need help with construction we call for professional services from a carpenter, plumber, or electrician. For physical health needs, we call doctors, nurses, and other specialists.

Clinical depression and anxiety disorders may overlap physical and mental health. Depression disrupts normal quality or function of life. Some purely physical conditions, like thyroid dysfunction, serious anemia, heart disease, diabetes, chronic pain, and so forth, can cause symptoms similar to clinical depression or anxiety. If you suffer, your first step should be to get an accurate diagnosis from a qualified physician.

Self-help books, like this one, can be effective resources, offering increased understanding, coping skills and support. When the need goes beyond what we can do for ourselves, we need to reach out for personal and/or professional help. We need to make informed choices. Here is a listing for some of the wide variety of people offering services.

WHO'S WHO ?

PSYCHIATRIST

Psychiatrists are medical doctors (M.D.) with special training in mental health and a focus on 'neuro-biological' disorders. They are licensed and certified medical specialists who diagnose mental disorders, and prescribe medication as needed to treat them. Counseling and psychotherapy may be offered, but a focus on psychopathology and medical treatment is the major part of most practices.

PSYCHOLOGIST

A psychologist, in most states, holds a Ph.D. or Psy.D. degree. This licensed professional will do an assessment and diagnose mental illnesses, but does not focus on medical treatment and, in some states, does not prescribe medication. Psychotherapy is used to treat patients, which involves listening and talking with them, and engaging them with varied learning, cognitive, and personality theories, and strategies.

SOCIAL WORKERS

This licensed professional has earned a master's degree in social work and has training in psychotherapy (listening and talking). He or she will focus more heavily on the social and societal issues that might affect individuals, and on using different social services and community resources to support improvement.

LICENSED COUNSELOR

These professionals focus on marriage, marriage and family therapy, or specialties such as Child/Adolescent services, Aging, Addiction, and others. There are also Licensed Clinical Mental Health Counselors, trained in psychotherapy, who focus on their particular specialty areas. All have earned at least a baccalaureate degree, and most will hold a master's degree, depending upon their state's requirements.

PASTORAL COUNSELOR

In addition to biblical training, pastors offer counsel, scriptural advice, and support. Depending on their training, pastors may use Christian adaptation of psychological treatments. They will not diagnose medical or mental conditions, or prescribe medications.

They refer to licensed mental health professionals for those services, and for in-depth treatment of major mental illnesses. Pastors and volunteer (lay) counselors can help refocus us on the spiritual dimension of our lives. With prayer and scriptural guidance, they offer comfort and support as we move toward healing and change.

THERAPIST

This is an umbrella term covering Psychiatrists, Psychologists, Social Workers, Marriage and Family Counselors, Addiction Counselors, and many other licensed or unlicensed, clinical or even non-clinical specialists. They may hold a variety of educational, and professional degrees (M.D., Ph.D., Psy.D., M.S., M.A.., B.S., B.A.), or a high school diploma, which is the legal minimum requirement for non-specified use of the term.

You may gain great therapeutic benefit by working with any therapist if their qualifications, skills, practice, experience, methods, and worldview accurately match your needs. Question the qualifications and scope of practice of any therapist you consider working with. Be sure that your needs have been accurately determined, and know your own goals and desires for help before starting any treatment programs.

LIFE COACH

Life Coaching is not therapy or counseling. It is focused on personal goals, like health, weight, increasing confidence, business success, and relationships or other voluntary changes in a client's personal life. Coaching seeks to clarify "what's happening now" by exploring specific obstacles, challenges, and choices of actions to achieve life goals.

Currently, there are no legal educational or licensing requirements to become a 'Life Coach'. Voluntary certification agencies such as the International Coaching Federation (coachfederation.org) seek to standardize general levels of training, performance, experience, and ethics, of credentialed coaches. Such professional groups could be a good place to begin looking for quality services.

There are, undoubtedly, some incredibly gifted life coaches, in different specialties, that provide clients with great success and satisfaction. There are also, undoubtedly, less qualified folks in practice too. Life Coaching services cannot substitute for mental health counsel or treatment.

PEER SUPPORT GROUPS

There are many groups such as those sponsored by the National Alliance on Mental Illness (NAMI). They offer, powerful resources, and many are available at no charge. Find more information about peer support at: www.nami.org.

Local church groups or ministries may also know of or facilitate Christian Peer Support groups. NAMI may also be able to refer to faith-based programs in your area.

FAMILY/FRIENDS/NEIGHBORS

No licensing agencies or regulations exist for these relationships, but they can be extremely therapeutic. Always use discretion when confiding in those nearest and dearest to you. Each of us has strengths, weaknesses, and "baggage" that may sometimes color our understanding or judgment. At times our best intentions may require a delicate balance.

Sometimes the words don't even matter in healthy, loving relationships. A warm hug, a willing ear, or companionable silence can be healing.

Remember, you are not alone. If supportive people are absent, God never is. He promised to be with us always, even to the end of the age.

STRATEGIES

Seeking help is a sign of wisdom, not of weakness. These strategies can aid you in selecting the help that meets your particular needs.

SEEK TRUSTWORTHY ADVICE

Ask people you trust, and who have had some experience with similar issues. They may help find potential therapists.

USE TRUSTWORTHY AGENCIES

There are many such agencies and here are some examples.

- Focus on the Family's Counseling Department can help locate Christian therapists in your area who specialize in treating similar difficulty. They can be reached Monday–Friday 6:00 a.m. - 8:00 p.m. (Mountain time) at 855-771-HELP (4357). You may need to wait for a callback, but they promise to be in touch as soon as possible.

- The American Association of Christian Counselors can link you with the Christian Care Network's directory of Christian mental health professionals, and ministry-based counselors who are credentialed through the Board of Christian Professional and Pastoral Counselors (BCPPC). Reach them online (www.aacc.net) or by phone (800-526-8673) Monday–Friday, 8:30 a.m. to 7:00 p.m. (Eastern Time Zone).

- The Honey Lake Clinic, in Greenville, Florida has been rated as the # 1 Christian mental health program in the United States. They offer 24/7 behavioral health treatment services on-site, as well as refresher programs to help with recovery from addictions. Contact: (855-524-3180).

- The Lighthouse Network develops faith-based behavioral health, life-impacting resources. The Lighthouse Helpline and Case Management services provide expertise in connecting struggling people to faith-based addiction and mental health treatment options. 24/7 Helpline: 844-LifeChange (844-543-3242), www.LighthouseNetwork.org.

HEALTH INSURANCE REFERRALS

Your insurance carrier may have a list of qualified providers in your area who are accepted by your plan for coverage.

LOCAL AND REGIONAL PUBLIC RESOURCES

Your local Mental Health Services or County Health and Human Service offices may be able to help in your search.

NATIONWIDE RESOURCES

- The National Alliance on Mental Illness (NAMI) is a treasury of trustworthy information and referral guidance and you can find them at www.nami.org.

- Check The American Counseling Association Therapy Directory on the Psychology Today magazine website: http://therapists.psychologytoday.com/rms/.

This site is also recommended: counseling.org/Counselors/ LicensureAndCert.aspx. This is a directory of state counselor licensure boards, with phone numbers and Internet address.

- The Substance Abuse and Mental Health Services Association, (samhsa.gov) provides information about treatment facilities and programs in the USA and US Territories for Mental and Substance Abuse Disorders.

Knowing the titles, specialties, and qualifications of potential helpers, and identifying good referral sources are important steps to finding someone to work with.

But, wait—there's more. You don't want just any well-qualified counselor; you need the one you feel is a good fit and can meet your specific needs. Important steps to take, and questions to ask that help to assure your best fit, are coming up. Stay with me.

SCRIPTURES FOR MEDITATION

"Bear one another's burdens, and in this way you will fulfill the law of Christ." Galatians 6:2

"So we being many, are one body in Christ, and individually members of one another. Having then gifts differing according to the grace that is given to us, let us use them: if prophecy, let us prophesy in proportion to our faith; or ministry, let us use it in our ministering; he who teaches, in teaching; he who exhorts, in exhortation; he who gives, with liberality; he who leads, with diligence; he who shows mercy, with cheerfulness. Let love be without hypocrisy. Abhor what is evil, cling to what is good. Be kindly affectionate to one another with brotherly love, in honor giving preference to one another." Romans 12:5-10

CHAPTER 13—WHO YA GONNA' CALL?

J.D. walked through the door stomping out his righteous anger with every step and bringing instant heat with him. He sat, silently glowering at his peers who held their collective breath.

With a sympathetic glance, T.S. said, "I guess we don't need to ask how your treatment team meeting went."

"No, T you don't need to ask. All my team wants to talk about is what's wrong with me. They're looking for problems, not progress. Why bother?"

This scene was part of an actual Recovery Skills group experience. Teaching in a psychiatric hospital, geared to follow a medical model of treatment, has been one of the most challenging, and rewarding experiences of my life. I chose to use this story because the answer to J.D.'s question might also be of help to you, as you consider a search for the right therapist to work with. I asked him to consider a different view.

TREATMENT TRIAGE

Focusing on what's wrong does make perfect sense—in context. For example, if you're suffering physical pain, you want to know if it's indigestion, gall bladder, or a heart attack. The leader of J.D.'s treatment team was a specialist who devoted years to education and medical practice in his field. A diagnostician has one goal, and that is to find out what's wrong, so that corrective steps can be planned.

As long as a patient remains in recovery, the medical team will watch carefully for any difficulties or complications. And that's exactly what we want them to do. However, once the biological concerns are addressed, do we want or need the same focus on potential negatives in emotions or relationships? Well, that depends.

Consider an injured MVP star for a major sports team. At the time of an injury, he wants great diagnostics and immediate, and watchful, corrective treatment. But after a recovery period, when he's easing back into practice (newly healed, yet weakened), with potentially rusty skills and shaken confidence, would he want the focus to stay on the problem? Or would it be better to switch into identifying assets and strategies for making the most of his remaining ability, to strengthen and build up his weaker game? Context is a major consideration.

J.D. decided to keep on trying to demonstrate progress with biological and behavioral recovery to his team, so their watchfulness could switch from negative concerns, to potential positives. He also planned to use assertive communication by asking for his team's help in identifying assets and strategies, and training him to make the most of them, as he worked to restore *his* game.

PERSONAL CONSIDERATIONS

How about you? Are you clear about the kind of help you need? Are you hyper-focused on what's wrong and seeing mostly weaknesses? Do you need help to identify your strengths and to make the most of them?

To gain the most benefit from outside support, in the best time, you need to find the right match. Once you identify potential therapists, it's time to fine-tune your search. Your mind-set is important. Growth and recovery are active pursuits—not passive surrenders. You are not a helpless victim waiting for an expert to rescue you. You are a full partner in the recovery process.

You possess, and you are using, wisdom and courage to act on your need to hire a specialist with the right skills and attitude. Forming a partnership, to work with you in support of your efforts and goals, is a move of strength, not a sign of weakness.

Interviewing is a part of any hiring process, and you can do it. Three to five telephone interviews of different candidates are suggested. You want to screen for the most favorable impressions, or screen-out an obvious mismatch, before making your first appointment.

Don't be dismayed, or inhibited in your search. Think of who you are. You are a survivor who has come this far. And, you are a much-loved child of the King! If your symptoms have you feeling overwhelmed and too shaky to interview in advance, then just go ahead and pick someone from your referral list and make that first appointment. You can use your first two or three sessions to interview and evaluate, as part of your selection process.

That first step, making the call, is incredibly important. Give yourself credit for taking it. Remember that you're gathering evidence of your successes and strengths. This is one of them. Write it down.

Don't fear that you will be stuck with the first therapist you see. There are no contract rules, and no legal obligation, or reasonable expectation to continue, if you aren't comfortable with a therapist. Good therapists will refer clients to other specialists if they aren't comfortable or feel they can't effectively serve a particular client's needs. You can make that same choice for yourself.

STRATEGIES

Here are some steps to help you reach your goals by getting the right kind of help.

Pray for wisdom and guidance and use a variety of questions to guide your selection of prospective therapists or counselors.

SUGGESTED QUESTIONS TO ASK

- Do you accept my insurance?

The therapist might not know your individual plan but they should know whether or not they could work with your provider.

- Tell me about your beliefs or worldview?

- What experience do you have working with my kind of difficulty?

- What is your approach to doing therapy with someone like me?

Can the counselor clearly define how he or she might help? Were varied techniques or programs explained? Were you given any choice in the approach? Can they give you a general "road map" to their plans? And can the therapist give you milestones for measuring progress, or an idea of how you will know when therapy is finished?

- Do you tend to direct or to facilitate?

Does the counselor encourage client dependence or independence? You will likely need both approaches at different times, but the best therapy encourages independence. Therapy is designed to help you find soothing, supportive strategies that you can activate and experience on your own.

- Is your therapist open to receiving feedback from you about what is, or is not, working? How about positive and/or negative feelings?

Good therapists will seek feedback from you. They need to know how you are receiving their suggestions, and how well you feel things are going. The language of defense can be painfully unproductive. Both therapy partners must share understanding and open communication.

- What types of things might you expect me to do between sessions? Is there homework?

If so, does it make sense to you? Is it reasonable? Are you willing?

- Does your therapist-candidate offer any guarantees or promises?

Be cautious. Healing is possible by the grace of God. It may be instantly miraculous, but more often you will need the will to change and to invest the necessary time and effort. How much time, desire, and determination will be required depends on who you are, what you're dealing with, and how many obstacles you need to over-come. Hope is real and should be inspired within you, but no one can set absolute time limits or unconditional promises about what improvement to expect.

- Will everything shared between us stay private and confidential?

If anyone is to be contacted or informed about any part of your work, you should know from the start. Patients knew that things said, in our classes, were confidential and would not be shared except for statements or behaviors that caused concern for their own safety and welfare, or that of others. Those would be referred for direct, immediate intervention.

- How are things like appointment cancellation or other difficulties handled? If you need to be away, what happens to my therapy? Are there options, like phone sessions?

- Ask: Do you think you can help me?

The therapist should express some confidence.

After all has been said, do *you* think they can help?

NOTES ON EXPECTATIONS

Research suggests that you can expect some shift, or hint of relief, within three sessions. If you don't sense any change or hope for progress within that time frame, speak to your therapist about exploring added or different approaches. If you are not satisfied with the response you'll need to consider a new therapist.

Keep in mind there will most likely be periods of some discomfort as you work on sensitive issues. Don't be surprised. Vulnerability is a part of the process, but you should be able to express those feelings and find support to continue. If you feel threatened, try to avoid becoming defensive. Be honest with your therapist and find a way to work through it. If you can't, then move on. But don't give up too easily.

MATTERS OF FAITH

Did answers to your questions align with your beliefs? Is your faith valued and respected? Did you sense compassion and optimism? Did you sense a real reason for hope, or did you feel a rush to judgment?

Remember, there are no winners in the blame game. Do not allow any real or imagined judgments to derail your positive efforts. You are much more than a diagnostic label.

THE BIGGEST QUESTION

Did their answers satisfy you? Training or experience in your area of concern is important, but you want to make sure you will feel comfortable with the helper you select.

This is not a complete list. You will have some questions of your own to add, but this is a good start. Potential counselors won't be shocked by your questions. If they are, it speaks to their own insecurities. Seeking the right helper is important. Pray as you prepare to search. Ask questions and listen to responses. Then, listen to your own heart about whether you have a good fit. God promised to answer requests for wisdom.

SCRIPTURE FOR MEDITATION

"Let the peace of Christ rule in your hearts, since as members of one body you were called to peace. And be thankful. Colossians 3:15

*   *   *

Reaching out for help is a sign of strength—not weakness. And, Building recovery skills requires *independent* as well as assisted work. We need both.

Chapter 14—Alphabet-Therapy Soup

Congratulations! You're still reading—and you're taking action toward towards recovery. You have more power than you may have given yourself credit for. We have talked about finding the right therapist, now let's explore the types of therapy you may want to adapt, with professional help, as needed.

Different models of therapy are often labeled by their initials. For example, a listing of CBT (Cognitive Behavioral Therapy), ACT (Acceptance and Commitment Therapy), and DBT (Dialectical Behavioral Therapy), can sound like ingredients for alphabet soup rather than effective, evidence-based treatment models for depression and anxiety. It's time to define the ingredients and check out these recipes for success.

Ted Geisel, writing as Doctor Dr. Seuss, could have been writing about the promise of Cognitive Behavioral Therapy when he penned this quote:

> *"Think left and think right, and think low and think high.*
> *Oh, the thinks you can think up—if only you try."*

COGNITIVE BEHAVIORAL THERAPY (CBT)

So, what is Cognitive Behavioral Therapy (CBT)? It's a short-term, goal-oriented treatment, with a practical, hands-on approach to problem solving. CBT proposes that it's our *perception* of events and situations that cause problems—much more than the events themselves.

CBT techniques equip us to confront and directly challenge negative patterns, or errors in thinking (working from the outside-in) to support positive change.

ACCEPTANCE AND COMMITMENT THERAPY (ACT)

Acceptance and Commitment Therapy (ACT) agrees that our thoughts (perceptions) about things, cause more difficulty than the things themselves. But, rather than trying to erase or directly challenge and resist our negative thoughts and feelings, this model offers a very different approach, (working from the inside-out,) for revision and improvements.

DIALECTICAL BEHAVIORAL THERAPY (DBT)

Webster's Dictionary offers these ideas about the term 'Dialectical':

1. The art or practice of examining opinions or ideas logically, often by the method of questions and answers, to determine their validity. This is logical argumentation.

2. The method of logic, based on the principle that an idea or event generates it's opposite, leading to the reconciliation of opposites.

DBT encourages clients to use logic for handling difficult, over-whelming emotions and thoughts by questioning them, and then applying opposites of thought or behavior, as needed to resolve or reconcile difficulties. DBT includes special techniques for crisis management. We will apply Do-It-Yourself strategies, based on DBT Crisis Management techniques.

BON APPETITE

Just as Tomato Bisque, Minestrone, and Cream of Broccoli are all vegetable soups, our Alphabet-Therapy Soup recipes offer unique tastes, for different appetites, and require different preparation. Our three therapeutic models all focus on cognition (thinking), and engage our behaviors in very distinctive ways.

We prize variety of menu selections in our kitchen space. We need a full menu of treatment options to resolve problems we may face in mind-space too. These three models are not the only ones we could explore, but they are representative of the most widely used, and highly effective, evidence-based approaches to therapy.

Research shows no significant difference in outcomes between therapy that focuses on a single, standardized cognitive approach and those that vary treatment, to fit individual needs. You are unique. So are the difficulties you may need to face. A single tool may not equally serve all tasks, and that's okay.

Before we dive into the how-to details of therapy, and how to make each of these distinct tools work best for us, let's take a big picture over-view. In his book, Cognitive Therapy Techniques In Christian Counseling, Dr. Mark McMinn outlined six active ingredients in effective, emotional healing. They are:

1. Trust, unconditional positive regard (empathy and emotion), and confidentiality.

2. Explanations, or ways to understand complaints, and guidance for building relief.

3. The ability to understand problems in new ways and learning new ways to cope with them.

4. Real hopes and a reasonable expectation of improvement that goes beyond mere wishful thinking. Confidence is crucial.

5. Success. We need to experience and recognize progress. Marking evidence of our success helps to keep hope alive, and bolsters the confidence we need.

6. Emotional investment and arousal is part of the process. It's unavoidable and it's valuable. It feeds motivation.

We have already attained some of these. For example: In prayer we experience total, unconditional love and acceptance. We can trust that we are heard, and confidentiality is assured.

I hope you agree that numbers two and three have been partially satisfied with what we have learned so far.

Hope should be blossoming in your heart right now. You are armed with real and practical strategies that you know how to use, and we have biological explanations of why and how we *know* that they work. We have reason for real confidence that improvement is not only possible—it's in process.

Our need to experience success is also partially satisfied by taking stock of all that we have accomplished so far. Look back in your journal to review the evidences of success you have been gathering. If you need another boost, give yourself credit for what you are doing right now. You have been faithfully reading and considering a lot of new information, and taking on new challenges almost daily. Bravo! Keep going!

Our emotional investment has paid off, so far. And there are *many* rich dividends still to come. It may, at times, feel like we're on an emotional roller coaster. We can be confident that our highs and lows will provide thrills, as well as chills, and that we'll be glad we took the ride.

In the coming pages, these six ingredients will continue to enrich and spice the flavor of our therapy 'soup'. Taste and see if you can identify them in the recipes we will explore.

PRELUDE TO THERAPY

Cognitive therapies are concerned with freeing the sufferer from faulty or distorted beliefs that get in the way of clear, rational thinking. This approach lines up nicely with Christian principles, as it directs us to compare our thoughts with truth. As believers, we have a trustworthy standard for comparison. God's Word is our source of truth.

"All scripture is given by inspiration of God, and is profitable for doctrine, for reproof, for correction, for instruction in righteousness." 2 Timothy 3:16

Ability to focus on the here-and-now has been called self-awareness, or "mindfulness". It's required for full engagement in our lives, and it's a key to cognitive therapy. We need to recognize errors of thinking, before we can check and correct, to re-align thoughts with truth, or to ask for help in doing so.

This focus isn't self-indulgence or un-Christian practice. It's the opposite! We're not talking about emptying our minds, or about getting stuck in a loop of personal philosophy. Support for in-the-moment awareness starts in the Old Testament. Identifying Himself to Moses, God did not say *"I Was"*, or *"I Will Be"*. He said… *"I AM."* Exodus 3:14

Connection with our God might include reflecting on lessons from the past. We may also share our concerns, and hopes for the future with God, but it's in the here-and-now that we reach out, and it's moment-by-moment we live in His grace.

We have been instructed: *"Be still, and know that I am God; I will be exalted among the nations, I will be exalted in the earth."* Psalms 46:10

I think that verse could serve as an outline for Christian mindfulness. Let's look at each aspect of it.

- **Be.** Just *be*. It takes practice, but we can learn to do it consciously. Even if, in this moment, you feel like a hot mess, you can still acknowledge that you're alive and loved by a perfect God.

- **Still**: We can quiet our 'busy' minds, with physical focus on this moment. Let's do it right now. Take a deep breath and release it with an exhaled prayer. Thank God. He is *with* us. Keep breathing that truth into your being.

- **Know**. Become aware of what's going on in our body/mind senses and remember, even if we feel out of control, we are fully within the control of our all-powerful God. He's *got* this!

- **He is God.** And because He *is* God we have hope, help, and unconditional, unlimited love for every moment of our lives. When we acknowledge and give thanks for those truths—**He is exalted**.

Whether you engage in a therapeutic process on your own or with counsel, it's going to be an emotional experience. As we explore therapeutic approaches and how to use them, you can be confident you're working with some of the most effective methods available. And, you have an absolute guarantee you will never be alone—God is with you.

STRATEGIES

When we are in emotional pain, we tend to focus on it. When healing starts, we can become aware of, and focus on positive benefits. Here are some steps to increase awareness of the positive healing that is taking place within you.

TALK THINGS OVER WITH THE LOVER OF YOUR SOUL.

Tell God in prayer what your thoughts are about all of this. Ask for wisdom and strength as you prepare to put it to use.

PRACTICE AWARENESS

Remember, we have two-way signal traffic between mind and body. We can start to quiet our minds, and our thoughts, with physical awareness. Try these techniques.

- Sit comfortably, with your feet flat on the floor, your back well supported, and your hands, (palms up,) in your lap.

- Close your eyes and take three or four deep breaths.

- Notice what you feel. Is your body hot or cold? Are your muscles tense? Can you relax them? Feel the weight of your body against the chair cushion. How is your heart rate? Is your breathing smooth, slow and even or do you notice irregularity?

- As you tune in to what's going on in your body, and become more relaxed, you may be able to slip into inner space to recognize some things about your emotions and the thoughts layered behind them. Don't judge anything, just notice, and keep breathing.

- When you're ready, open your eyes and describe your experience, to yourself and to your God.

You can write this description in your journal, or just ponder it. Do what works best for you. This exercise may change your perspective or inspire more specific prayer. As you gain experience, you will be able to accomplish this 'mindfulness' in more informal ways, without needing to sit with eyes closed for a five-minute exercise. Our responses change when we quiet our minds enough to recognize them.

RECORD AND REVIEW YOUR PROGRESS

Make a journal entry. Review your progress. Record your new ideas, goals and questions. Remember that your journal becomes evidence of your success. It will help support you to build even more success with recovery as you continue. Give yourself credit and thank God for insights or comforts you found.

SCRIPTURES FOR MEDITATION

As we explore new strategies, we can celebrate promises like these:

"Trust in the Lord with all your heart, and lean not on your own understanding. In all your ways acknowledge Him, and He shall direct your paths." Proverbs 3: 5-6

"Therefore do not worry about tomorrow, for tomorrow will worry about its own things. Sufficient for the day is its own trouble." Matthew 6: 34

"...And surely I am with you always, to the very end of the age." Matthew 28:20

"…Weeping may endure for a night, But joy comes in the morning." Psalms 30:5

Dear Reader, we are getting closer to morning.

CHAPTER 15—CHECKS, CHALLENGES, AND CHOCOLATES

When we're stressed, depressed or anxious, we may seek a quick fix with extra activity or with unhelpful self-prescribed substances. My drug of choice is chocolate. One friend would say the same about coffee. There is nothing wrong with the tasty choices my friend or I might enjoy, but if we looked to these treats for long-term pain relief, or real solutions, we would be sadly disappointed.

GETTING *REAL* RELIEF

There is no quick fix substitute for the genuine Cognitive Behavioral Therapy (CBT) work of self-examination and correction. If we become aware of negative thoughts and irrational beliefs, we can check the evidence and make correction.

Some may still be wary about developing awareness and self-evaluation skills because they believe that it's not good to focus too much on self. But, honest examination has been advised in both old and new testaments. For example, Lamentations 3:40 instructs: "Let us examine our ways and test them, and let us return to the Lord."

Once we identify painful ideas, we can choose more realistic, healthier ways of thinking. We might challenge irrational beliefs, replacing them with more accurate views. For example: "Because I am depressed right now, does not mean that my faith has failed, or that I am a *bad* Christian."

Our Lord is our greatest, perfect, example. Jesus grieved when He heard of John The Baptist's execution. He wept over Jerusalem, and with Mary and Martha over the pain felt when Lazarus died. We read of His emotional agony in Luke's account of His prayer in the garden just before He was betrayed.

Mary and Martha also felt amazement and joy when Lazarus was raised from the dead. Joyous amazement definitely followed Jesus' resurrection. *Feelings change.* That's an important point to remember.

METACOGNITION (THINK ABOUT THINKING)

Some common negative thoughts seem to invade automatically. News Flash—We are not responsible for ideas that slide across our minds. Negatives surround us, picked up like static, in this fallen world. We are responsible for deliberately 'tuning-in', fixating on, or believing the negatives. They can seem to grow in the dark. So let's look at them in the light of truth and challenge, revise, or dismiss those that don't fit. Our abilities to think about thinking, to challenge and control our own thought processes, will improve as we use them.

Considering what we now know of the power of our thoughts to shape and form the very structure of our brains, spending time and energy this way seems like a very reasonable investment.

Good assessment starts with questions: Are your thoughts in alignment with facts? How about with the truth of God's word? If we want to renew our minds, we need to understand our thoughts and feelings and evaluate them.

Faith, love and joy are meant to be our 'default' settings. This may sound simple, like accepting a gift. In some ways it *is* that simple. God's love is a free and unconditional gift. Faith is also a gift of God. And, joy is the result of both. We can accept these treasures, with thanks. Beyond acceptance, it's in *maintaining* an "attitude of gratitude," and in *applying* our gifts that we seem to have trouble.

With so much competition for our attention in this world, we need prompts to use our gifts, and not just occasionally.

Remember, our brains allow us to define and rate our own ideas of importance, and to set our own minimum response thresholds for those ratings. If we assign importance and high rates to questionable things we risk missing others that are equally, or even more, valuable to us.

Let's get "Meta." We need to filter everything that seeks entry into our hearts and minds. That's clear direction. We need to monitor our thoughts and stand ready to check, challenge and adjust or replace thoughts that are out of alignment with truth. That takes disciplined choice, and relentless application. Hmmm, these are the same qualities required for re-programming neural pathways. How exciting!

AUTOMATIC NEGATIVE THOUGHTS

Automatic Negative Thoughts can cause mental pain. In his book *Healing Anxiety and Depression,* Dr. Daniel Amen named them ANTs and compared them to ants at a picnic. One or two may not be too bad, but an invasion can spoil everything. Some of the most common ones have been identified. We need to catch and resist these errors. (Direct CBT Challenge.)

CHARACTERISTICS OF ANTS

Here are some of the main characteristics of ANTs and a few suggestions to consider. Do any apply to you?

- **Over-generalization**: This type of emotional thinking allows us to expect that if a thing happens once, it will happen with everyone, every time. Tune in to your self-talk. Are you thinking in these *absolute* terms?

"She's always late."

"You do that every time."

"He never listens."

"No one really cares about me."

"Everyone disrespects me."

"I'll never be able to do that."

If these are your thoughts, check, and challenge!

- **Negative Focus**: Focusing on the negatives may seem like a survival tactic. We think we are staying alert for danger. But remember, we're setting up filters and response thresholds. We tend to find what we're seeking. If we keep our attention on the negatives we can filter out, and totally *miss* the good things in life.

- **Predicting the Future**: Predicting future negatives is an error in thinking that invites painful bites. None of us can control the future, and we can't *know* it either. That's a good thing. If I had known what difficulty lay ahead, I wonder if I would have attempted some of the journeys that led through pain en-route to some of the greatest joys of my life. "Fortune telling" seems to be at the heart of much anxiety, and takes a toll on our health (via the mind/body connection).

- **Mind Reading**: This error is especially dangerous to relationships. God is the only one who can truly know what's going on in the thoughts and hearts of man. As close as we would like to feel, and as much as we might think we know our loved ones, we cannot read each other's mind. Simple indigestion might explain the sour look you noticed as you entered the room.

These thoughts are examples of Mind Reading:

"She doesn't like me."

"They think I'm wrong."

"He's mad."

We can get stuck in vicious cycles with this error. It's painfully frustrating to approach a loved one and ask, "What's wrong," only to have them expect us to read their minds: "If you really cared, you would know." Ouch! Mind Reading is risky, whether you are the one attempting to do it or the one who expects it of others. When in doubt, check things out.

- **Judging Feelings as Facts:** Feelings are powerful—but they are not facts. Feelings change, and are not always accurate. Accepting negative feelings as fact, without first checking to be sure we have our facts *straight*, risks painful, and costly error.

- **Guilt**: The Holy Spirit uses the conscience, to guide us into wisdom. But, "guilt tripping" too often simply trips us. We risk sabotage when we tack guilt onto (otherwise positive) goals:

"I have to lose weight."

"I should call my sister."

"I must get organized."

"I ought to get up."

Just framing things that way makes me want to run. How about you? I have not had much success using guilt as a motivator to avoid "Forbidden Fruit" either. If we yield to temptation, we may feel guilty about our failure or weakness. If we resist it, we're martyrs. That's joy pollution. Instead, we can thank God for forgiveness, and for our ability to re-frame perspectives and to walk in freedom, by His grace.

- **Negative Labels**: These are vision blockers. Once we slap a label on them, we can no longer see people or situations as they are. Instead, we see the label, and toss everyone and everything wearing it into the same lump where it's impossible to separate accurate details, qualities, causes or solutions. If we can't see a problem or situation clearly, we can't improve or resolve it either.

- **Getting Personal**: Taking things personally, or mixing this view with other thinking errors, sets up a perfect storm for anxiety and depression. You are not the target, or the cause, of all bad things that happen—any more than you, (all by yourself), could be the recipient or the cause of everything right and good in the world, even if you would like to be. Personalizing this stuff makes us miserable. We multiply pain and reduce hope. A friend gave her students a Q-TIP and taught them a strategy named for that humble token: "**Q**uit **T**aking **I**t **P**ersonally." I don't know where she found the idea, but I love it.

- **Blame:** Playing the blame game robs us of strength and power. This error is one of the biggest, "baddest" of the ANTs. Blaming creates victims. Victims are not in control. Victims don't have power to change things. Don't be one. Being accountable and taking responsibility for our thoughts and actions is necessary, but we can only learn from mistakes, make corrections, and avoid them next time. Getting stuck in a guilt trap reinforces negatives, and distracts us from finding solutions. At the risk of repetition (you have heard this before): *There are no winners in the blame game.*

Tune in to your self-talk. Listen to that inside, running commentary. Think about your thinking. Ask yourself questions to clarify things. Then pray. Check and challenge thoughts that are clearly errors, or that don't align with God's truth.

SCRIPTURES FOR MEDITATION

King David shows how to use our greatest power-tool, which is prayer. He said, "Search me, God, and know my heart; test me and know my anxious thoughts. See if there is any offensive way in me, and lead me in the way everlasting." Psalm 139:23-24 (NIV)

Paul described the kind of thinking we need. This verse is worth repeating:

"Finally, brothers, whatever is true, whatever is noble, whatever is right, whatever is pure, whatever is lovely, whatever is admirable—if anything is excellent or praiseworthy—think about such things." Philippians 4:8

Jeremiah, an Old Testament author, was aware of, and saddened by, errors in thinking and action that led to the destruction of Jerusalem. But even in the ruins, he found hope and reason to trust. We can too.

"'I remember my affliction and my wandering, the bitterness and the gall. I well remember them, and my soul is downcast within me. Yet this I call to mind and therefore I have hope: Because of the Lord's great love we are not consumed, for his compassions never fail; They are new every morning; great is your faithfulness." Lamentations 3:19-23

Now, that's better than chocolate!

CHAPTER 16—ANTs AT YOUR 'PICNIC'

Speaking of picnics, I'm not suggesting that formal, or even informal, Cognitive Behavioral Therapy (self-help) is a walk in the park. To be honest, learning to monitor and check our thinking, and to bring it into alignment with our truth and values, is hard work. It's not a one-time assignment either. But, it *is* possible. The more consistently we practice, the more success, and ease we will find, as this becomes our new, hard-wired, pattern.

If you are in crisis with painful ideas, thought checking may best be attempted with a counselor. Wisdom dictates, asking for help is a sign of strength,—not weakness.

As we reviewed Automatic Negative Thoughts (ANTs), we understood Dr. Amen's metaphor of a picnic where one or two ants are not a problem, but an invasion is serious. We 'get' that, right? Now that we're aware of, and can identify, ANTs, let's challenge, and get rid of them.

ANT INTERVENTION

For real insects, I use a two-stage defense in my kitchen. Stage one is a plug-in ultrasonic pest repellent, advertised to prevent infestation of ants by sending out sound signals that are not audible to the human ear, but are very irritating to 'critters'. The sales copy promises they will drive undesirable pests away.

Stage two is a powerful spray to kill off any insects that get through my first line of defense. It's working, so far.

But our concerns are 'ANTs' that invade our thoughts, not my kitchen. For those we will use a Six-Step CBT Process:

1. Notice problem thoughts and emotions.

2. Find and identify Automatic Negative Thoughts.

3. Dispute them.

4. Find the hidden Core Beliefs that feed the ANTs.

5. Dispute untrue or dysfunctional Core Beliefs. Declare correction!

6. Maintain progress.

Core Beliefs are not always easy to identify. Discovery may seem like peeling an onion. We begin in the top layers of our "onion-hood" with an examination of self-talk, that silent internal conversation that we all have with ourselves. These are early clues.

Automatic Negative Thoughts are next, and still fairly close to the surface. As we recognize and deal with these, we reveal deeper, and deeper layers of thinking, feeling, and believing. Repeated patterns of Automatic Negative Thoughts are clues to underlying core beliefs. We need to become Detective Inspectors, acting on our own behalf. Here's an example:

1. Jane worried about her housekeeping. Since she started working, she just couldn't seem to get everything done. She felt inadequate.

2. Next, she felt guilty about being too busy to enjoy a relaxed time with friends and family, and wondered if they felt neglected or abandoned. She gave up "me time."

3. Spending less time for self-care made her feel grouchy and unattractive.

Her thoughts of being inadequate, guilty and unattractive, contributed to her feelings of being unlovable. These three ANTs formed a pattern, and offered clues to Jane's core belief that she had to *earn* love, by measuring up to arbitrary, standards. She thought she fell short.

The core belief that these Automatic Negative Thoughts revealed were not aligned with Jane's Christian faith. It was an unhelpful, dysfunctional conclusion, and begged to be disputed. The truth is that God loves all of us *unconditionally*. We don't have to earn it, and we never could. God loves us because He *is* love. We're all invited, and it's a come-as-we-are feast!

STRATEGIES

Even when life is not a picnic, we need to be mindful of ANTs. Here are some practical ideas to help do that.

- Notice when negative thoughts are "bugging" you. Identify ANTs.

- Consider using a Daily Mood (or Thought) Journal to help you keep an accurate record. Notice hurtful thoughts. Write them down as soon as possible. If you wait, you may miss important details and patterns, and only recognize a sad, general case of the "blahs" or worse.

- Ask questions: Is that thought helpful or hurtful? What triggered it? Did something happen, or change? Was this just a vague *"sort-of"* feeling or a specific negative emotional shift?

- Consider your brain/body connections. What physical cues can you identify? (Did breathing or pulse change? Any tension or weakness?)

- What are you telling yourself? Check that internal dialogue. What's your self-talk about right now?

Congratulations! You may have just identified some Automatic Negative Thoughts (ANTs). Describe them as clearly as you can. Write them down.

Keep asking questions:

- What's the source for these thoughts, and that message?

- Are you re-playing old scripts?

- Are they lines you created, or someone else's ideas?

- Are you voicing fears?

- Can you separate thoughts and feelings?

- Is there evidence of truth for these thoughts? You could try listing the evidence. Is it convincing? Does it line up with the values and core beliefs you consciously hold?

- Will things get better or worse if you continue thinking this way?

• When we recognize an Automatic Negative Thought, we need to take immediate and purposeful Action. Take them on one-at-a- time. ANTs can be smashed by the weight of evidence, and/or sprayed into oblivion.

• Think of a way to re-frame or re-state your troubling thought in a less damaging, more helpful way or to completely discredit it. Look for evidence that can discredit errors and *use* it. We can agree with humorist Ashley Brilliant's observation. He declared that he might not be perfect, but that parts of him were excellent. This is true for us, too. We could try taking some positive action to go with more positive thinking.

A HOMEMADE REMEDY

I described a two-stage defense against ants in my kitchen. This may be useful as a metaphor for our mental picnic too. My first step was to plug in an electronic repellent, using ultrasonic-sonic signals to drive pests away. Could we try a variation of this approach? Perhaps we could saturate our area with positive sonic (audible) signals to similar effect. Could we speak our truth out loud? Could we tune in to positive, uplifting music, or listen to favorite recordings? Could we *double* the enjoyment, and the benefit, by singing, humming, or playing along?

The next step, in my kitchen, was to use spray at the first sight of any pests that evaded my sonic line of defense. For these mental ANTs, we need a very different kind of pesticide. Try this (figurative) brand of ANT *S P R A Y*:

Stop.

Pray & Play: Pray for wisdom, then play back the thought to clarify it.

Review the evidence: Is there truth? Is this thought helpful or hurtful? Try to be objective. Based on the evidence, how would you judge this thought if it were about someone else that you loved?

Argue your case. Use your self-talk ability to talk back to the offending ANTs. If the thoughts are wrong or untrue, crush them with the weight of evidence that proves it. If they get too loud, or come too fast, silently yell, "STOP!"

No matter how painful your negative may be and even if it does, at least partially, apply: align your thoughts with truth. When in doubt, check things out in God's word. He says you are His treasure. He says that His mercies are new every morning. So even if you can't completely discredit an ANT with evidence, you can still crush it with truth… that you are forgiven, unconditionally loved, and free to start over with a clean slate every morning.

Yield to a healthier, helpful, truthful conclusion. Yield to the loving guidance of the Holy Spirit.

SCRIPTURES FOR MEDITATION

If it feels as though you've engaged in a battle—be encouraged:

"For the weapons of our warfare are not carnal, but mighty in God for pulling down strongholds; casting down arguments (imaginations), and every high thing that exalts itself against the knowledge of God, and bringing into captivity every thought to the obedience of Christ." (2 Corinthians 10:4-5 (NIV)

Strongholds can be defined as many things to different people. Anything that has enough of a grip to keep us in our misery, or prevent us from freely and fully entering the peace and grace of God, could be a stronghold. Faulty core beliefs certainly qualify.

We are not alone in the battle, and the banner over us is love. We may be wounded, but we are promised to that we will stand with the winner of the war. I hope you enjoyed our metaphorical picnic. Get comfortable with these CBT skill-building tools. We're getting ready to enter a major ACT of recovery.

CHAPTER 17—ACTS OF FREEDOM

Cognitive Behavioral Therapy (CBT) and Acceptance and Commitment Therapy (ACT) are two of the most successful evidence-based treatments available. They are related, yet very different. C.B.T. is direct confrontation. A.C.T. is mental martial arts.

If you enjoyed the movie Independence Day, watching humanity win against the alien invaders, you may have walked out of the theater (or got up off the couch) with a renewed sense of optimism and hope. You had renewed faith that we can powerfully unite (against a common enemy), in the brotherhood of man.

There is an appeal to the idea of doing battle against an enemy. We can imagine ourselves as heroes. Like David, we stand against the Goliath of Depression and Anxiety. We know this Goliath has legions of ANT warriors ready to invade through any breach in our defense.

We cannot completely block Automatic Negative Thoughts (ANTs) from infiltrating our lines. If ANTs are few and fleeting, they are a nuisance not a danger. Real trouble comes when the enemy does not just pass by – but decides to dig in and occupy our precious, hard-won territory, enlisting our diagnoses, or other circumstances in the attack. That's when the war must begin. Or does it? The answer is, "Yes"; "No"; "Maybe"; and "Sometimes."

Some battles absolutely *do* need to be fought. If our thoughts are captured by lies (as with the ANTS), we need to resist—and go all-in with everything we have. A believer's weapons of resistance are found in the truth of God's word.

Other battles may require surrender. For example, it would be futile to fight this realization: "…I am not perfect. I can't do it all, please everyone, or fix everything." If surrender to that truth is painful, take comfort in a bigger truth, which is "God *is* perfect. He loves me. He's the one I need to please. He is for me, and is with me. So, I can keep on—keeping on."

Still, other battles may be resolved through negotiation. For example, "I can't fight this right now, but I can recognize it as a hurdle in my path, and I can ACT to clear it, for the next single step in my race." Wisdom for winning comes in knowing the differences in strategies—"when to hold, and when to fold," and which to use for our greatest benefit.

WHO'S IN CHARGE?

Before we engage our adversaries, we need to seek strategic command. The chain of command for believers is obvious and, our first sensible action is always prayer. Be encouraged. Even when we're not sure of what to pray for, we have help.

Romans 8:26-27 says, "In the same way, the Spirit helps us in our weakness. We do not know what we ought to pray for, but the Spirit Himself intercedes for us through wordless groans. And He who searches our hearts knows the mind of the Spirit, because the Spirit intercedes for God's people in accordance with the will of God."

We live in a 'fallen' world, full of hardship, injustice and pain, but also of beauty and blessing. There are times of war and times of peace. The Old Testament advises: "There is a time for everything, and a season for every activity under the heavens: a time to weep and a time to laugh, a time to mourn and a time to dance." Ecclesiastes 3

There will be times when tears are the most appropriate response to a situation. If we never shed tears, we risk feeling drowned in our own un-expressed emotions. There are times when we need to ask for help. We were not designed to face all of our battles as an army of one. There is strength and wisdom in reaching out for help. There will be times we do need to stand in battle against the cause of our tears. And yes, at times we may have to stand solo—but we are never truly alone. God has promised to always be with us.

POINTS TO PONDER

After a hard-won victory during the war of 1812, American Navy Commodore Oliver Hazard Perry said, "We have met the enemy—and they are ours." That quote starred in one of cartoonist Walt Kelly's "Pogo" comic strips. Celebrating the first observation of Earth Day, 1970. Pogo, (the possum) commented on the careless trashing of planet earth, and on the need for better stewardship, by famously paraphrasing Commodore Perry's quote. Pogo said, "We have met the enemy and he is us." Pogo's warning still applies today. We must guard against trashing 'inner space'. We need to give very careful attention, avoiding trash in our self-talk, because our brains will believe whatever we insist on telling it.

In our CBT battle with the ANT invasion, we used questions as weapons in our arsenal. As we prepare to ACT we need to answer a few *different* questions.

- How much attention does this deserve? Will attention be helpful or hurtful?

- If I need to do battle, how sure is the ground I stand on? Is it rock solid truth, or is it quicksand that will take me down more quickly as I struggle?

- What tactics are needed? Do I stand and deliver toe-to-toe and blow-by-blow against negative thinking, or should I use different strategies?

Imagine the differences between Boxing and Aikido. Picture Rocky Balboa vs. Apollo Creed as they faced off, trading blows. Got it?

Next, imagine Steven Seagal, using fast, fluid, moves, not to present a wall of resistance, but to deflect and re-direct the flow. He turns his enemy's own energy and movement against him.

If CBT challenge is an effective "'stand and deliver" boxing strategy, then Acceptance and Commitment Therapy (ACT) may be more accurately viewed as "Emotional Aikido." We don't know where our next struggle may take place, or what method we will need to use in facing it. We need skills in both types of defense.

In his book, *The Happiness Trap*, Dr. Russ Harris' presentation of ACT explained that in our quest for happiness, we try to banish bad feelings. But the more we try to do that, the more bad feelings multiply. That's the trap. Struggling to deny, smother, or ignore certain negatives, can feel like trying to run through quicksand. In this struggle we move better, toward solid ground when we understand and express our needs, using Emotional Aikido instead of blunt force opposition.

We have met the enemy, but we don't have to become one of our own. We can face our thoughts, beliefs, and feelings with honesty, commitment, ACTion, and good communication. If we do, we can pick up the trash, take out the garbage and defend against ants.

THE MYSTERY OF CONTROL

The people I know who are most uninhibited, and successful in expressing emotions and getting their needs met, are all under five years old. Infants and young children don't worry too much about controlling their emotions, they just let 'em' rip, making their needs and desires known clearly. I have sometimes wished I could do the same, without sacrificing my precious adult dignity, of course. How about you?

We dignified adults want to feel that we do have control. Some of our earliest lessons teach us we *should* have control of our feelings. We invest time and effort to do so. And it works, some of the time. At other times, that struggle for control can sink us. Long before 5th grade, we hear that we should, "Stop being afraid," or "Don't be a crybaby." Or, "Be a big girl/boy—it can't hurt that bad."

As adults, we learn that "Stuff happens," and that we should "Cheer-up," "Don't be so sensitive," or "Get a grip." We tell ourselves, "It is, what it is—move on." In fact, we can become so conditioned to the need for control (to "suck it up"), we may even try hiding legitimate physical injury.

As an environmentally conscious adult, I commuted to work by bicycle for a while rather than driving. I recall an accident that happened one day, on my way home. After a spectacular crash, I was humiliated. I pulled myself up, bleeding and limping, to my feet, straightened my dignity as best I could, and then slapped a fake smile on my face. I announced, "I'm okay" when asked if I was hurt or needed help. The twisted frame of my bike, multiple body-aches and pains, and my silly wounded pride, made for a long walk home. Can you relate?

Dealing with embarrassing visible injuries is difficult. Handling our own invisible, emotional pain can be even harder, especially when we play the roles of both victim and self-judge.

RISKY BUSINESS

Sometimes, as we seek resolution of our problems, our solutions become problems themselves. For example, scratching an itch is a harmless reaction so long as it is an occasional and fleeting thing. We all know constant scratching increases irritation. And injuries can compound difficulty by becoming infected. We can't begin to heal until we stop scratching. It can become a vicious cycle. The same risks apply when we try to deny emotions. Trying too hard to be happy can actually be dangerous to our wellbeing. We don't need to banish all negative thoughts or emotions. We just need to learn how to *handle* them. We may be able to control our feelings for a short period. But, in the long run, we need better solutions.

In his book, Dr. Harris described some popular emotional control strategies.

- Fight or Flight. This involves denial, stuffing (pushing down) our feelings—or trying to escape them by hiding or running away.

- Zone out—or "Numbing." We may try drugs, alcohol, excessive sleep, or getting crazy-busy as we attempt to numb, or shut off our feelings.

- Distraction or Confrontation. We may eat, binge-watch television, or go shopping to distract ourselves, or we may decide to take on the battle by arguing against reality with self-judgment, by saying, "I shouldn't feel this way." All of humanity has faced these continuing struggles. King David asked: "How long must I wrestle with my thoughts and day after day have sorrow in my heart? How long will my enemy triumph over me?" Psalm 13:2

- We may try "taking charge." This is giving ourselves orders to "snap out of it." We may even try being a bully, calling ourselves names such as "idiot," or tripping ourselves with guilt by saying or thinking, "You're pathetic. Get a grip."

If control strategies are moves of resistance, are they wrong? Not always. I bet we can all recognize a few that we have used. Like scratching an itch, emotional control strategies can be practical and effective in the short-term. But, they should be used sparingly, in situations where they really can work, and where using such a strategy doesn't contradict our values.

Control strategies are not okay when misapplied. They can't work with grief, and they don't work when such a strategy conflicts with truth or with what we truly value (such as mindlessly 'eating or drinking your stress'—while valuing sobriety and good health). Control strategies are unhealthy if used too often in mental battles.

Since emotional control strategies are not always best, what's left? Let's focus on what we *can* control instead of what we can't. We cannot always control our emotions, but we can control our behaviors. We can learn to ACT. Acceptance and Commitment Therapy offers much promise, and we can learn to use it in self-help.

STRATEGIES

The ACT process requires action. Consider the ideas presented here, and prepare with these suggestions.

- Pray for understanding as you review.

- Continue in your journal—and in reviewing your positive scripture affirmations

In the next chapter we'll learn the specifics and seriously consider the additional (alternative) strategies of what I'm calling "Emotional Aikido." You can become a champion.

SCRIPTURES FOR MEDITATION

"No temptation has overtaken you except what is common to mankind. And God is faithful; He will not let you be tempted beyond what you can bear. But when you are tempted, He will also provide a way out so that you can endure it." 1 Corinthians 10:13-14 (NIV)

The Greek word for temptation can also mean testing. It's easy to understand our desire to avoid, control, or deny feelings of defeat, hopelessness, and sadness, when we're faced with painful trials. We would rather fight or hide than to admit them—but those feelings are part of being human. We can benefit by letting go—asking for wisdom, and for help with our responses. We have a sympathetic, understanding advocate who also said:

"...and be content with what you have, because God has said, "Never will I leave you; never will I forsake you." Hebrews 13:5

"And we know that in all things God works for the good of those who love him, who have been called according to his purpose." Romans 8: 28

CHAPTER 18—HOW TO ACT WHEN UNDER ATTACK

In the classroom, Anne had time for one deep breath before the rushing attack began. John's face flamed as he ran, reaching toward his intended victim.

She breathed her reminder: "Okay, I need to stand easy. I move *with* him."

Matching her moves to his, in both speed and direction, she stepped in and then gently pushed. His momentum carried him in a new direction as she turned the opposite way, running for help.

"Great work." The coach said, "Remember, the goal is not to stop the movement—but to re-direct a charge so that danger moves away from you. You're buying space for positive moves. You won't get that by trying to fight the force of attack."

Practice exercises in 'Managing Assaultive Behavior' (M.A.B.), were part of the training required each year of all level-of-care staff at our hospital. Reviewing the Acceptance and Commitment Therapy (ACT) protocols, reminded me of that training since both put emphasis on redirection of different forces that may come against us.

Although ACT therapy doesn't apply to physical actions, it is a powerful strategy for emotional attacks we sometimes face. In memory, I still hear the M.A.B. instructor's summary: "The purpose is not to oppose, but to re-direct the energy of an attack, and add positive action. Move toward your goal, and away from injury.'"

Applied to coping with depressive episodes, this seems akin to "Emotional Aikido." I hope the analogy of mental martial arts is helpful. We need to understand and define the terms. Let's break down the acronym:

ACCEPTANCE AND COMMITMENT THERAPY (ACT)

ACCEPTANCE

Acceptance does not mean agreement. It simply means acknowledgment. Acceptance, in this context, means recognizing that a negative something, physical or mental, exists and making mind-space for it.

For example, an injury may leave a survivor with limited movement or a missing limb. He may never *agree* with his circumstance, but he can accept it, and adjust to make the best of what he has.

Attempts to deny ignore or argue an injury would not be helpful. Expanded perspective sees the injury as a part of life, but certainly not all of it. Here's some good news: If we recognize and accept the existence of honest injury (rather than fighting it), we can change the function and power of negative thoughts and feelings.

COMMITMENT

Commitment means refusing to do anything or to move in a direction that is not consistent, or in alignment, with the values that give our lives meaning and purpose. It also means determination to do those needful things that *are*.

TAKING ACTION

Taking effective actions, guided by our values. Move toward your goals.

A DEEPER LOOK

If we mapped out our example of the hospital's M.A.B. training, using the ACT format, it could look like this:

- (A). An unexpected aggressive physical threat was made. Anne did not deny, ignore or argue with it. She accepted the danger, and expanded her perspective to assess, to recall past instruction, and to prepare herself for action.

- (C). She thought of the hospital's recovery mission, and safety policies. She connected with values. Given differences in physical strength and stature, she realized direct physical confrontation, (a struggle,) would prolong and increase the risk of harm to the patient, to herself, or to both of them.

- (T). She took effective action—'by going with the flow' of movement until the opportunity came to deflect the attack. She did this with a harmless push using the patient's own momentum, as she made a speedy retreat in the opposite direction toward safety.

This physical action happened quickly. There was no time for planning, or careful analysis. Anne relied on training and practice, which is the reason for annual M.A.B. classes.

APPLYING THE PRINCIPLE

A similar sequence can play out mentally. Negatives may arise by surprise, and may feel extreme. When we recognize imminent, emotional attack, we want to ACT quickly, moving in accord with our values, and toward a goal of recovery. The more we practice, the more smoothly effective our actions become.

START WITH MINDFULNESS

Get physical. Notice the details in what you are doing and feeling. Feel the rhythm and flow of your breathing. Scan your body for sensations of comfort, position, movement, and tension. Then, shift your focus to your thoughts and your actions. Thoughts are words—in stories we tell ourselves about our lives. They may be true, false, or something else.

Opinions, attitudes, ideals, and judgments are stories about how we see things in our life. Plans, goals, and values, are stories about how we want to live it. These thoughts (the words or mental pictures) about the events of our lives, are not the events themselves—although they may feel like they are. The story is not the actual experience any more than a dreamed beach scene would have you waking up with sand between your toes.

When we believe our thoughts and feelings, we mentally 'weld' them to our reality. If they are true, and support our values, it's fine. But, stories that are not true, or that conflict with our values, are not helpful. Those cause pain.

If we stick with those negative thoughts, merging them with our version of reality, we give them undeserved, attention and obedience. Dr. Harris calls this a state of "fusion." These thoughts may frighten us. Feeling threatened, we may urgently want to get rid of them—rather than face them, which leads to a struggle for control, and into quicksand. Bring on the mental martial arts.

DE-FUSE NEGATIVES

We can choose how to use these thoughts, but first, we have to "de-fuse" them. When we are in "fusion" with our thoughts, as Dr.

Harris explains it, we believe they are all-encompassing, absolutely true, and terribly important. We need a more accurate point of view.

We can start by expanding our perspective. Mentally step back far enough to see the negative thought for what it is. It's a story, we tell ourselves. It's not necessarily real. We can reduce its power by recognizing it accurately in our self-talk. For example, "I can't handle this" becomes—"I'm having the *thought* that I can't handle this."

To gain even more distance, try adding words to your phrase: "I *notice*, I'm having the thought that I can't handle this." Try it—and feel the change you gain by mentally stepping back, to make space in your perspective. A little distance can make a great difference.

The attention, and degree of serious belief, we give to our thoughts makes them powerful. We can change that. We tell ourselves stories about who we are, how we are, how valuable or able we are, and what that might mean to others, and to events in our lives, all of the time. Tune in to your self-talk to hear the dialogue. Check the scripts of your thinking. Ask for wisdom.

In the drama of our emotional lives, editing is possible and important. Begin with recognizing a story (emotional thought, response, and self-talk) for what it is—a story. Try giving your stories a title. Then decide if you want to be entertained by them, edit them a bit, or completely revise things. Once you recognize, and acknowledge thoughts as stories you can move past old scripts and use your God-given creative ability for change. Repeated thoughts form links adding to, or shaping, the structure of our brains. Editing skills can be learned. We can use them wisely, guided by the Holy Spirit.

MORE IDEAS FOR BECOMING *UN-STUCK*

Great directors know the drama in a scene can be changed by things such as dialogue, movements, scenery, lighting, and by altering the musical score. Would the movie, *Jaws* have been as memorably frightening if the music, used to pace the attack scenes, was the "yellow brick road" tune from the Wizard of Oz? No. That relentless, racing, heartbeat rhythm of the shark's approach sent powerful emotional signals.

What would happen in the theater of our minds if we put our scariest emotional stories to lighthearted music, or used the voice of a non-threatening, silly, character in the dialogue of our negative self-talk? A mismatch may break the spell, and offer more room for perspective.

This is not intended to minimize, or make fun of real difficulties, but to offer a bit of mental distance that enables us to break their grip on our energies and attention. We need positive action, to break feelings of being helplessly *stuck* in a sad, bad plot. The next time you recognize this pattern, pray first, then try one of these ideas.

EVALUATE EMOTIONAL THINKING

Once we have de-fused negative emotional stories we can assess them. The stories exist. We don't have to prove, disprove or defend them, just ask if the thoughts are helpful or not. If they are helpful, go ahead and use them. If not, then recognize, accept their existence, and label them. Do whatever editing is needed for your mental story—and then move on to the next (physical) step.

COMMIT TO ACTION

Choose an action that agrees with your values. Notice your motivation too. Doing the right things, for the wrong reasons won't be so rewarding.

The action you decide on doesn't have to be revolutionary. It could be something as simple as taking a hot shower, or a short walk. The important thing is that you make a commitment to values-guided action, and then *do* something.

For example, if you've lost your appetite, are feeling sick at heart, stuck in a bad/sad story, and wrapped in a blanket of despair, maybe, (after implementing acceptance, de-fusion, and expansion), your next step might be the physical act of making chicken soup.

Maintaining health is a meaningful act that is in agreement with your values. So, get busy. Be fully engaged as you wash those vegetables and prepare the chicken and stock. See the colors, and feel the textures of those carrots. Smell the celery, or onions. Hear and feel the peeling and chopping as you prepare. Make soup as if you have never done it before in your life, mindful of every detail and sensation. Be fully focused and prepare to enjoy. Savor both the experience, and the final flavor. That's making ultimate use of the recipe for Alphabet-Therapy soup!

THE CLUES ARE CUES TO ACTION

Start the process with mindful awareness of your self-talk and your experiences. If you are dealing with ANTs, crush them with positive evidence or use SPRAY. If it's something more, be ready to ACT.

Don't ask questions such as "Why am I feeling this way?" "What did I do to deserve this?" or statements like, " I can't take this." These thoughts invite struggle and judgment. They are not helpful.

Anxiety seems most often focused on the future. Depression seems focused on the past. A great quote has been attributed to *Family Circle* cartoonist Bill Keane and, some say, to Eleanor Roosevelt. Either way, the wisdom is profound. "Yesterday is history. Tomorrow is a mystery. Today is a gift of God, which is why it's called the present."

If we're stuck in the past, or the future, we are disconnected from the present moment. But the present is truly all we have. It's where we live. We're robbed of our joy in the moment if we disconnect from the experience of it.

Good News:

There is good news in all this. Our joys increase when we connect to meaningful, values-guided action. This doesn't happen accidentally. We can't make significant changes or improvements in our lives by reading about them, any more than reading or dreaming about a tropical paradise will put us on the beach.

To feel the sand beneath our feet, and the warmth of the sun—to hear the music of the waves, and taste the salt in the air, we need to take action. We need to get up and *go*. We need to consciously change our patterns of thinking and action. Reading is a good start, but it can't take us all the way to our goals. Living the experience can.

ACTION STRATEGIES

Put knowledge into action.

1. TRY DOING AT LEAST ONE PLEASANT ACTIVITY EVERY DAY.

Be sure it's something you can be motivated to do because of its importance, meaning, or true value to you. Don't be engaged with hidden agendas of control, escape or avoidance.

2. TAKE IT EASY AT FIRST.

Do lunch with a friend, take a walk in the park or enjoy your favorite music. Look for other simple pleasures. Do this thing as if you have never done it before.

3. ENGAGE FULLY

Do it fully, and be consciously engaged. Put total focus on what you are doing—on what you can see, hear, touch, feel, smell, or taste. You are entering the two-way traffic of inner space and <u>your body</u>

can help direct your mind. If your thoughts drift, and you catch yourself not paying attention, no worry. That's normal but it means you have disconnected. Thank your mind, and your Maker, for your ability to notice and then re-engage. When you focus on what you are doing, in the moment, you strengthen skills of being mindful and boost your enjoyment too.

Dr. Hayes described the "Happiness Trap" as similar to a paper cage. He explained: "...Although it appears so—the cage isn't really a barrier for the human spirit."

4. OUR STORIES NEED NOT DEFINE OUR REALITY

While we may build emotional 'paper cages' that seem true, and strong enough to lock us in with pain, and to limit our abilities, they are illusions. As believers we can rely on the Holy Spirit, to guide us. The Spirit can break us free, and give us wings. Ask for the help you need.

5. KEEP UP WITH YOUR JOURNAL ENTRIES

Once you have completed your ACT for this episode, note your success. Not only did you survive a moment of crisis, but you are gaining skills and strength every time you put a coping strategy to work. You no longer need to feel completely helpless or hopeless in the face of difficulty. You are becoming an expert on when, and how to handle it, and you are building a whole collection of tools you can use. Congratulations!

SCRIPTURE FOR MEDITATION

In Psalms 139:17-18, King David expressed his thanks. "How precious also are your thoughts to me, O' God! If I should count them, they would be more in number than the sand. When I awake, I am still with you."

God's thoughts for us are more in number than the sands of all of the seas. That's better than any "beachy" dream.

CHAPTER 19 — RIDING A STORM EMERGENCY PREPAREDNESS

Personal catastrophes, trials, and losses have been described as "storms of life." They can certainly feel similar. For example, October 2016 brought devastation from Category 5 Hurricane Matthew. Hurricanes Harvey, Irma, and Maria, hit with sudden and terrible impact in 2017. There may be many more recent storms reported by the time you read this. The timeless truths of this chapter are that sudden destructive forces can occur in all areas of life and that, while we can't control them, we can do some preparation to help us survive them.

Horrific events started with low-level atmospheric depression, and dark clouds gathering over open Atlantic water. Then, within hours, storms grew into monsters, flooding Texas, and punishing South Carolina, and Georgia. Islands were destroyed in the Caribbean, and Puerto Rico suffered unprecedented levels of loss and devastation.

How do the appearance and characteristics of a hurricane relate to depression and anxiety? Can we learn anything from the analogy that might be useful for coping with 'emotional storms'?

SUDDEN RISK

Ordinary circumstances may create stress or waves of difficulty. It can start with a few dark clouds gathering on our mental horizon, and a lowering of expectation or mood, but no real need for alarm. Then, we can suddenly find ourselves blown away by gale force winds of fear, grief, regret, or some other negative emotion that seems out of proportion to our current difficulty.

Does this mean there is something radically wrong with us? Have we had a major breakdown of our faith or moral fiber? No, absolutely not. Depression and anxiety react to changes in our experience, our expectations, our biology, and atmospheric pressure within our inner space. Those reactions can be swift, seeming to hit with hurricane force. If we know this in advance, we won't be completely unprepared.

STORM WARNING

Hurricane winds can tear up trees, rip structures apart and damage or demolish everything that stands in their path. Mayhem and destruction follow the storm's progress as it makes landfall. As terrifying as they are, the winds, despite the immediate force of their power, may represent a lesser danger. In epic storms the greatest threat to life often comes in floods, in a storm surge and lingering rains. Up to 90% percent of reported, storm-related, deaths come by drowning in these floods. Emotional storms cause similar risks. To experience sudden, overwhelming emotion is referred to as "'flooding'."

We all live in hurricane country, within inner space, because we all live in a fallen world. Some of us may be at more frequent risk than others—but all of us will face this type of storm at some time in our lives.

The hurricane force of a depressive episode can shake us to our core. Things we thought were rock solid may be uprooted or torn apart. We face on-going risk as the waters rise with our tears, fears, and flooding emotions. We need to find refuge. Thank God emotional and spiritual refuge exists. David said: "For in the time of trouble He shall hide me in His pavilion; In the secret place of His tabernacle He shall hide me; He shall set me high upon a rock. Psalm 27:5

Being in God's pavilion, hidden away in His tabernacle, high upon *the* Rock assures our ultimate safety. Hold on to that vision and to the absolute surety of His love through every storm. With our souls secured, we must do our best in preparation to weatherize our physical, and mental, spaces.

When a natural disaster hits, we seek cover. As immediate danger passes, we attempt the first steps of recovery, like checking our surroundings to get out of harm's way. Next, we do physical assessments, of ourselves and others, and apply first aid. Then, we grab emergency supplies, and look for clean water, food, shelter, and other necessities.

EMERGENCY PREPAREDNESS

Learning first aid, planning an evacuation route, and stocking supplies are life-saving ideas that are worthless unless they are put into effect before a crisis strikes.

The moment of crisis puts us in survival mode. This is not the time to attempt new learning, or creative thinking. We need to know what to do, and how to do it quickly. This truth applies equally to physical and mental (emotional) emergencies. When trouble comes, we instinctively send up prayers for protection and help. God promised that He always hears us, and He offers help, not condemnation. So, pray first, and then *move on*.

We can develop Emergency Plans for mental and emotional, as well as physical, storms and disasters. Emergency plans for inner space might look a bit like this:

1. Identify a place of immediate shelter.

2. Learn to do a personal assessment.

3. Know how to treat shock, and apply first aid.

4. Stock up on emergency supplies. Strategies and resources are metaphorical bandages, splints, and braces. Learn to use them effectively.

After the first hurricane blasts have passed we are still at risk of "flooding." If your emotional crisis sent you into dangerous or risky circumstances, stop, and go to safety. Choose any private and secure location. For example, shaking, weak knees most likely don't belong on the ladder you were using when this storm began. Driving may be good to avoid right now. If there is a temptation you normally find hard to resist, this would be a good time to avoid known sources. Trembling hands should probably not continue fine motor tasks (especially with sharp tools). The first reactions to overwhelming emotional crisis can feel like physical shock.

GET GROUNDED

I used to be confused by the term, "grounded." It sounded a bit too "New Age" for me, until I understood more of the principle. An electrical current needs to be grounded to flow safely. Using a different analogy, in high winds or on rough seas, I need a securely grounded anchor I can cling to. The same principles hold for emotional storms and raging seas.

You know where I'm headed with this. When our worlds are shaken, and floodwaters rise, we need to be grounded on the Rock. Have we failed a test of faith if we are shaken in the moment of crisis? No! But, we may need an emergency strategy.

We are God's living, physical temples. In crisis, we need to get out of the emotionally saturated environment of inner space, and allow our bodies to experience the external, natural ground on which we stand.

GROUNDING STRATEGIES

After prayer, one of the best ways to feel grounded is to get physical. Take a deep breath to a slow count of four. Hold it for another four-count, and then exhale to a count of seven.

At the end of each exhale, vocally add "Aha!" or "Ha ha" (whichever seems good to you). That final expression will remove the last traces of stress-filled dead air, and make room for fresh inspiration. Repeat this three or more times. Then, keep breathing normally and focus on the physical world, until you feel less 'blown-away' by your thoughts and emotions. Then, with increased awareness:

- Look. Notice, and try to describe five things you can see. Do it so well that a blindfolded person could picture them accurately.

- Listen. Notice five different sounds you can hear. Describe them.

- Touch. Notice five things you can move, or feel. Focus on their texture, weight, and other details. Put your description into words. The more you can focus on these details, the more the exercise enhances a calmer grounding effect.

- Stand up. Push your heels into the floor, or the earth. Focus on the effects of gravity on your body. Slowly shift your weight, rocking from your right foot to your left. Notice the changes in muscle tension, weight distribution, and other sensations as you move. Get out of your 'head'. Focus on your body for now. Sensing the body can help to calm our minds and emotions via the two-way traffic function of our neural network.

Thank God, even in the midst of the storm, you can still notice the sights, sounds and the feel of your physical environment. Trust that God is right there beside you. As you feel more 'grounded', you may notice that the flood is not rising fast as it was.

In your emergency plan, include an action list of things you can do to take stress levels down, to provide comfort and to help you survive, without making things worse, until calm is restored. Having an action list, adding these skills, and practicing in advance, provides those metaphorical bandages, splints, and braces for your emergency, mental, first aid kit.

D.B.T. APPLICATIONS

Dr. Marsha M. Linehan developed *Distress Tolerance Skills* as part of her Dialectical Behavioral Therapy (DBT) program. If you're hit with deep pain, in a dangerous emotional crisis, you might need a bit of "benevolent piracy" to force your attention in a different direction. Some of my students' favorites have been excerpted and adapted for self-help.

IMMEDIATE DISTRACTION

- Cry. It may seem counter-intuitive. Cry to feel better? Yes, sometimes it helps. Tears and laughter are both cathartic. They can clear your system of a lot of stressful emotion in a hurry. Don't be afraid that once you start crying, or laughing, that you won't be able to stop. You will stop eventually, and probably feel better because of the release of stress hormones. You will clear them out quickly and then, you might need a nap.

- Grab an Ice Cube and squeeze. Hold on for as long as you can stand it.

- Take a Cold Shower. Use the coldest temperature you can stand. Get in quickly.

- Sing. Give your song the same explosive energy you would invest in a scream. You will feel similar relief with a different spin. Pick a song you can suddenly belt out at full volume. Look for lyrical encouragement too. The words can mean so much. Will you choose Hard Rock, Contemporary Christian, or Folk Songs? You could try the Hallelujah Chorus, or Kelly Clarkson's anthem, "What doesn't Kill You Makes You Stronger," or join Mandisa's chorus, "You're An Overcomer." It's up to you.

Put full force and volume into your choice. If you're shy, sing in your car, alone in the shower, or sing into your pillow. It's all good. You can even turn a song into a prayer. God hears every cry.

Singing activates multiple parts of the brain including memory, as well as auditory, movement, and language areas (if the song has words). Singing also activates the reward centers of the brain, increasing dopamine, so you feel better. This stress reliever offers instant access, and complete portability. It's free, and it's effective! Don't let concerns about the quality of your voice stop you. It's joyful noise we're after, even if it begins in tears. Worry and worship can't occupy the same space, and time, in our minds or in our mouths.

- Move. Kick a ball, stretch, run, or crank up the music and dance. *Do something.*

- Get out of the house. Walk or drive. Observe nature, or watch people. Note their dress, behaviors, facial expressions or other features that catch your eye. How many have brown eyes or blue? Enjoy their energy and laughter. Realize you are not alone on the planet.

- Do Chores. Turn on your mindfulness and commit to action. Distract yourself with healthy activity. Walk the dog; make chicken soup; or stomp recycled boxes.

- Do something for someone else. Call someone, volunteer to help with charitable work, sweep a neighbor's driveway or rake leaves, take someone to lunch.

- Use your senses to soothe yourself. Make a list of sensory pleasures you are willing and able to enjoy. In moments of need, you might not be able to think of a thing to do, so do your thinking in advance and keep an idea list handy.

Keep it simple. For example, light a scented candle. Bake with cinnamon. (You can keep a ready-to-bake treat in the freezer for such a time as this). Take a bubble bath. Listen to music or sounds of nature, and really savor the sounds as you listen. Get a massage. Stop and smell the roses. Enjoy Art, or *create* some. Adult coloring books are satisfying too. Enjoy Rocky Road Ice ice-cream (unless sugar is your enemy).

- Give yourself a hug. Better yet, give someone else a hug. If no one else is close, give a stuffed animal or your pillow a hefty squeeze. Psychologist, A. Goodheart, recommended her wonderful "Charlie Bear" for this purpose. He is huggable and washable, absorbs tears, muffles screams, inspires conversation, and keeps secrets too. Charlie's cousin sits on my bed, surprising and delighting visiting grandkids.

Therapeutic pleasure doesn't have to be costly. If you're alone, and can't afford a massage, but you crave the comfort of pressured body contact, try rolling on an exercise ball while you sit or lay on it in varied positions. You could also go vertical by placing it between your body and a wall, and then press in as you roll around the room.

It's been suggested that we each need a certain number of deep daily hugs for good health. Hugs and massage were unavailable (and not appropriate) in our classroom, so the exercise balls got some real workouts. Imagine adult patients happily rolling along the walls of a long hospital corridor. It was fun to watch, and comforting for those involved. It was a happy experiment, and it worked.

If you can't afford a bouquet of roses, buy just one. Get to a garden, a florist, or to the floral section of a grocery store, and breathe deeply.

Have fun, and be creative with this list. Add to it on your better days. Keep it in your wallet or posted on your wall for ready reference. Make a commitment to do one or more of these activities when you feel the immediate need to lighten a dark moment.

Thank God that He makes so many wonderful possibilities for us. He enjoys our enjoyment of His gifts. Let's use them. When calm returns, make a note your success. By the grace of God you are still standing. You chose to take action, and you weathered the storm. Rejoice!

SCRIPTURE FOR MEDITATION

I heard about one woman's answer, when asked to name a favorite Bible verse. She said: "…And it came to pass." I looked it up. That phrase is used 182 times in scripture, with two interpretations, which our gal gave as equal reasons for loving this phrase:

1) Whatever is ordained by God, will happen;

2) Whatever happens—will pass.

King David wrote beautiful words of encouragement:

"God is our refuge and strength, A very present help in trouble. Therefore we will not fear, Even though the earth be removed, And though the mountains be carried into the midst of the sea; Though its waters roar and be troubled, Though the mountains shake with its swelling." Psalms 46:1-3

CHAPTER 20 — INSTANT VACATION: MENTAL BREAKS

A small child may cry, for no apparent reason. Their little body can shake with heavy, heartbreaking sobs. Then, something shiny, fun, or tasty appears as a distraction and smiles break out on a face still wet with tears. Have you ever seen this phenomenon?

I'm pretty sure every adult who has ever cared for little ones has shared this experience. We've also seen or used the magic of distraction to relieve a small child's pain from falls, shots, and other "boo-boos." No matter the cause of original tears, once we have taken care of any real injury, our instinct is to comfort the wee ones by taking their attention off of the mad-sad-bad thing, and turn it in a happier direction.

As adults, we are more guarded, and less transparent about it, but we too have painful, wrenching, emotional moments, sometimes without apparent reason. Distraction could help, as we saw in the last chapter, but we may be more reluctant to seek comfort. The good news is that we don't have to wait for tears, or for others to intervene. We can comfort ourselves by redirecting our attention. Here are a few extra ideas for distraction and inspiration:

MUSIC THERAPY

This is well known for its positive effects. It can alter brain chemistry by decreasing stress hormones, and lifting spirits. It can be soothing and relaxing, or energizing and stimulating. DIY music therapy involves finding music that lifts you, or soothes and relaxes you, and then putting it to deliberate use, as needed.

Experiment. Find music that works for you. Write song titles in your journal. Expand your options, and don't limit your choices. When you've found the right music for different needs, consider making CD or mp3 copies (for personal use only—not for re-sale). Record your songs in the order that does the best job of raising your spirits. Label and list them by category so you can identify and go-to these selections quickly.

Amplify positive results by actively engaging more than just your ears in the song. Sing along, dance, play an instrument, clap/tap out the rhythm or consider joining a drum group. Make a whole mind/body experience of it. Enjoy!

CINEMA THERAPY

We have all experienced movies that made us cry, or laugh—cheered us up, or calmed us down. If it's a good show, not only will we be distracted, our thoughts will be directed to emotional outcomes within that story.

Can a movie really be therapeutic? Several therapists believe so and books have been written on the subject that explain the theories and offer lists of recommended titles. *Reel Therapy*, by G. Solomon, and E-Motion Picture Magic, by B. Wolz, are just two examples.

Some movies offer practical idea-gifts for our mental first aid kits. *Finding Nemo* is an example. No matter how confused, lost or frightened Dory felt in troubling circumstances, she kept chanting encouragement—"Just keep swimming." Her mantra has been added to my self-talk library. It's a power tool I can use for comfort and motivation as I visualize those scenes.

The Greatest Showman is another favorite, for the messages in the story itself, and for the music. *Google* the lyrics and review the chorus of "*A Million Dreams.*" When you consider the love expressed in the lyrics of "*From Now On,*" and then re-direct thinking to a spiritual rather than romantic target, you suddenly enter soul-stirring worship! This one may lift us from feeling lost in the dark to new heights of encouragement, and take us right back home—to the arms of our beloved Father. We become like the prodigal sons and daughters we may have been, or felt ourselves to be. Whew! Popcorn anyone?

LAUGHTER

Scripture tells us, "A merry heart does good like medicine, But a broken spirit dries the bones." Proverbs 17:22

We recognize laughter as the product, or evidence, of a merry heart. But did you know it *causes* merry heartedness too? It's true! Laughter has been credited, in several research studies, with health benefits such as:

- Strengthening our immune systems

- Improving breathing

- Increasing arterial blood flow

- Aiding, digestion and sleep

- Helping adjust blood pressure and blood sugar levels

- Relaxing muscles

- Reducing pain

- Even burning a few extra calories.

Laughter is such serious medicine that it has been included in pain management programs, cancer nursing protocols, psychotherapy sessions, and many other applications. A quick Internet search on the topic will list hundreds of research reports and articles about the benefits of laughter for physical and mental health.

If you enjoy physical contact, and have a willing and appropriate partner, tickling is a fabulous method to stimulate laughter—for both the tickler and the one being tickled. If you are not comfortable with physical contact, or if it's not appropriate when you need it, that's okay. It's not required for laughter.

Sharing lighthearted social interaction with others is perhaps the most common way to get your spontaneous laughter prescription filled. And it's the most fun. Join the conversation! Laughter is contagious, like yawning. We can share this gift.

There are ways to stimulate laughter through humor even if you don't have company. Try going to a park and watching children at play. Try watching a funny movie, enjoy a humorous TV show, or recorded presentation. Go to a comedy club performance, or read humorous books and comics. Toys or costume elements can be effective. When is the last time you gave yourself permission to visit a toy store? "Tickle Me Elmo" is an older but still happy prop, if you can find one, and some puppets are hilarious).

Train your mind to look for humor in every-day circumstances including advertising errors, or weird road signs, or funny incidents. Remember that as you tell your brain what you want it to find—it will begin noticing and seeking it out for you.

How can we find laughter when depression robs us of humor appreciation? I asked this very question, since our patients were often stuck in that situation. Humor is a powerful coping tool, and yet some folks seemed unable to find the 'funny' in anything they viewed through clouds of depression. Seeking answers led me to research—

and to unexpected resources. I learned that laughter and humor are not the same things, and that you *can* have one without the other. The benefits of laughter can apply even when it's intentional, rather than spontaneous, with no humor required.

Laughter, for no reason, is practiced in groups such as the Laughter Clubs sponsored by the World Laughter Tour (www.world laughtertour.com) and in Laughter Yoga classes (www.laughtery oga.org). These can become incredibly effective therapy. Trained and certified laughter leaders facilitate groups through a variety of exercises in sessions that combine the benefits of laughter with the social support of other like-minded souls. The consensus is that simulated laughter leads to stimulated laughter (with health benefits), and to greater social connection. And that can be life-changing.

Abraham Lincoln said: "With the fearful strain that is on me night and day, if I did not laugh, I should die."

Speaking of social contact and its life-changing potential—the next chapter will shine more light on the subject. It's important. Keep reading!

CHAPTER 21— SOCIAL SYNERGY: PLUG INTO POWER

*"Anxiety in the heart of man causes depression—
but a good word makes it glad." Proverbs 12:25*

The sea breeze whipped strands of hair across her eyes. She didn't notice. Skirt fabric fluttered then wrapped around her hips and legs as she stood, unaware, near the edge of the Marin Headlands. Wavelets slapped the rocks, hundreds of feet below, and backed away again, leaving them slick, as if washed in a sea of tears. She didn't see. Traffic sounds and tourist voices faded away—as she was sucked deeper into her private tunnel of pain. She was alone. No sound. No feeling. No hope.

"My God, what a beautiful day. Isn't it? Look at that!"

A man's voice boomed beside her. Her startled senses snapped to attention. Forced to look, she suddenly noticed the colors he pointed out. White sails flashed over blue water, as a regatta approached the Golden Gate. Bright sun winked on the wave tops. She heard the cries of gulls, diving and soaring on a breeze she could now feel. Excited voices, and children's laughter carried sounds of life. He was right. It was beautiful. Stepping back she realized—she couldn't die today.

Misty-eyed, Rita, told of the wonder she experienced. This man had appeared, out of nowhere, and his words snatched her from the brink of suicide. When she looked, he had vanished in the crowd of tourists. She thought, perhaps, he was an angel who had suddenly appeared at the last second of her endurance. Who knows? One thing we can know for sure, simple words saved a life that day. Social contact, human connection, has that potential every day. And we have the power to engage.

*   *   *

I read a great story of one student's response to a difficult question. When asked to define darkness, he said the best way to really understand the dark was to experience light and then to know its absence. A similar contrast might illuminate our understanding of social engagement. Disengagement illustrates isolation. We know isolation as a common, troubling, even dangerous, symptom of major depression.

I have known days of illness or injury when I wanted to avoid others. I didn't want to spend my fragile energy, or to expose anyone else to my woes. I didn't want to expose myself to others' potentially poor opinion of my appearance, or performance. I just wanted to find a comfy corner to hide in, with my misery, until it passed. I wanted to say, "Wake me when it's over." Can you relate?

There are big differences between being alone, being isolated, and being lonely. We can all benefit from some quiet time, alone with our thoughts, or in solo activities. Being alone is only a problem if it's involuntary, or if it goes on for too long, and leads to isolation or to prolonged loneliness. These are different, and can be dangerous. Let's take a closer look:

SCIENCE AND STORIES

Isolation is a classic symptom of depression, and it may relate to personal protectionism, an attempt to limit exposure to conflicting views or judgments. It may seem like a good plan, and it might even work in the short term. But, in the long run, it's not a good idea. In fact, rather than protecting us, isolation can be dangerous. It has been noted to be a health hazard.

I have read that isolation and loneliness can contribute to high blood pressure, heart failure, breast cancer, accidental injury, sleep disturbances, and a host of other difficulties, including dementia. Hundreds of studies confirm these risks. Isolation increases risks for developing depression, and it compounds the pain of those who are *already* depressed. It is both a contributing cause of depression, and a classic effect.

That's a double punch that could knock us down for a count. But, we can flip this view by engaging opposites. If isolation rains these woes down upon us, then social connection may offer showers of blessings. Do you want some examples? Here are a few good ones: longer life, lower blood pressure, healthier hearts, reduced risk for breast cancer, fewer accidental injuries, and a host of other benefits, including sharper minds and memory. Plus, connection offers the opportunity for more love, and laughter to reach us even if we are in the shadows. So, we need to fight back. Unless we're in viral quarantine, we need contact.

Is "being down for a count—but fighting back" an appropriate metaphor for what we need to do? I think so. It's a choice that we sometimes struggle to make. Depression can rob us of our strength and energy. It can sap our motivation, distract us from our positive goals, and breed the desire for protection and isolation, which compounds our weaknesses. If we want to experience the fullness of life again, we must get up, get out, and get *with* others.

We may feel helpless, physically and mentally, and resist the sheer effort it can take to break out of this pattern. It is a vicious cycle, but take heart. We have more power than we may feel at any given moment. We do have choices, and we always have help—when we remember to ask for it.

"For I am the Lord your God, who takes hold of your right hand and says to you. Do not fear I will help you." Isaiah 41:13

Is it a struggle? Yes, and sometimes it's a big one. Is it worth the effort? Yes, without a doubt. Now we know *why* we need to launch into the positives of building or rebuilding social connection. Next, we'll review how to do that.

THE FIRST PRINCIPLE: WE ARE NOT ALONE

I recall students who entered my life-skills class carrying a lonely load of judgment, and doubt about their chances for recovery, and their prospects for the future. For some, lock-up in our forensic psychiatric hospital seemed to be a living enactment of the lines carved over the gates of hell, as portrayed in Dante's Inferno—

"Abandon hope all ye who enter here." Without hope, isolation seemed reasonable and safe. But, as we have discovered, it is not.

One class session began with this question. What do you have in common with Abraham Lincoln, Winston Churchill, and Michelangelo? The answer—a struggle with mental health issues in the form of major clinical depression.

Learning about the struggles many great people endured, and their amazing achievements in spite of it all, was an eye-opening experience for folks whose vision had not progressed beyond their present, personal predicaments.

Famous survivors of depression have shown that falling into a pit is not necessarily the end of our journey, unless we choose to stay there. As long as there is breath in our bodies, there can be hope in our hearts.

Dante's quote didn't fit our recovery curriculum. It doesn't fit yours either. We can take encouragement from the stories of people who have survived, and often thrived, despite their struggles with depression. National and world leaders made the list, as well as current celebrities. Their stories and strategies may help. We can profit from sharing ideas.

BUZZ ALDRIN

Buzz Aldrin's inspirational landing on the moon, in 1969, highlighted his career as an astronaut. He grappled with depression and alcoholism after this historic feat, and once said he couldn't recall ever sharing his pain with another male friend, or confiding in anyone about his struggle to hold life together.

He overcame his fear of stigma, and went on to serve as chairman of the National Association of Mental Health. Mr. Aldrin recognized that seeking help, and staying connected with others were important elements of his recovery.

TERRY BRADSHAW

Terry Bradshaw: was a famous quarterback for the Pittsburgh Steelers. He is a retired hall-of-fame star, and a current sports analyst and entertainer who went public with his struggles in the '90s.

In interviews, he has commented on the beauty of medications that work. He said that because of his happy-go-lucky personality, people found it shocking that he could be depressed. Terry credits his faith for getting through rough times.

In his book, *Keep It Simple*, he explains his coping strategies include focusing on the positives, seeking the joy in each moment (mindfulness), and sharing as much pleasure with others as possible. He advises that we stay connected with people; to always make sure dear ones know that you love them. He reminded us that we all need a hand to hold, and a heart to understand.

WAYNE BRADY

Wayne Brady is an American actor, singer, comedian, and television personality who battled depression alone until he finally sought help. He commented on the problem of being a man who has depression and the perceived social taboo to talk about it.

He stressed our need to overcome the stigma, and to speak up, asking for the help we need. He said, if we did that, we might help others get help too.

WINSTON CHURCHILL

Winston Churchill served as the British Prime Minister, during the Second World War. His depression was so severe and recurrent he named it his "black dog." That's a useful metaphor for examining the effects of depression. Dog bites are painful, but dogs can be trained, and controlled. And, at least to some degree, depression can be too.

Churchill battled his black dog by engaging in meaningful work, and by using his artistic painting, and writing skills as refuge. His famous advice given in 1941 is apt for us today. He said, "Never give in, never give in, never, never, never...."

DWAYNE "THE ROCK" JOHNSON

Speaking of his depression, Dwayne has said that knowing you are not alone is one of the most important things. He reminds us that we're not the first, and we won't be the last, to go through depression.

He has urged that we not give up hope during dark times, but hold on. He stresses the importance of faith, that there is something good on the other side of pain.

ABRAHAM LINCOLN

Abraham Lincoln, the 16th president of the United States held the Union together during the US. Civil War, and was responsible for the emancipation of slaves. He survived major depressive breakdowns, which included statements frightening enough for friends to form a suicide watch.

He once wrote, "I am now the most miserable man living." How did he cope? Lincoln's sense of purpose, his faith, and his determination were the keys to his survival. He used humor as an antidote to depression. He told jokes and funny stories to boost his spirits and said, "If it were not for these stories, jokes, jests, I should die."

My short list also includes such luminaries as:

- Samuel Clemons: Mark Twain (American writer)

- Charles Dickens (Author)

- Lady Gaga (Actress, Entertainer, Singer)

- F. Scott Fitzgerald (American author)

- Hulk Hogan (Wrestler)

- Charles Spurgeon (aka "The Prince of Preachers" 1800's Baptist)

- Stephen King (American author)

- Meriwether Lewis (American explorer—Lewis and Clark expedition)

- Isaac Newton (British physicist)

- T. Boone Pickens, Jr. (American oil tycoon)

- John D. Rockefeller (American industrialist)

- Charles M. Schulz (American cartoonist)

- Bruce Springsteen: "The Boss" (American singer/musician)

- Oprah Winfrey (American talk show host—celebrity)

- Ashley Judd (Actress)

Notice these names include males and females, historical heroes, musicians, celebrity entertainers, creative authors, artists, business giants, and others. Depression can affect any of us at any time, and most likely has touched us, or *will* touch all of us, at some time in our lives.

This is a seriously abbreviated, incomplete and random listing. A quick computer search will tell their stories and reveal hundreds more. You are not alone.

COMMUNICATION = CONNECTION

In a classroom experiment, I asked for a volunteer to test whether or not we can be within sight of each other without communicating. Our volunteer was convinced that he could do it. He stood silently, facing the class with a military stance. Attention! He avoided eye contact, put his 'poker face' on, and he waited. One and a half minutes later he breathed a sigh of relief, smiled, and sat down.

After just 90 seconds of close observation, the group described at least seven non-verbal messages received from our stoic volunteer, which clearly communicated his initial confidence and determination to succeed, and then his growing discomfort, embarrassment and impatience, followed by his relief and satisfaction. He was surprised by the variety and accuracy of the observations.

We should not be surprised to learn that others can, and do "read" us. We are wired for connection and we communicate, with or without deliberate intention.

Communication creates a connection. We need accuracy. Accidents, and guesswork can be risky or painful. Communication is the key to knowing we are not alone.

It is possible someone might need human contact more than a person who is at the bottom of a pit of depression. Maybe. But, while all of us want a social connection for a healthy life-balance, enrichment, and enjoyment, it is critical in the process of recovering from depression. You may ask, "Why should I consider breaking the silence about my depression? I don't want to complain or bother others, and I don't want to be judged by them either." Read on...

IT'S OKAY TO SPEAK OUT

There are good reasons for speaking out. First, if we want to be understood, we have to let people know what's going on. If we expect mindreading, or even good guesswork, we're setting ourselves up for disappointment. Depression is difficult to deal with, and even more so if you feel alone. You can find encouragement, and understanding by confiding in others. You can also find the freedom to simply be who you are, and how you are, and to ask for what you need. You may need a ride to your appointment; help in finding treatment, or in making a crisis plan, or something else.

Second, if you are struggling with depression, friends and family are most likely curious and aware that *something* is happening within you, and that it probably isn't good. They are already "reading" you just as my class read the unspoken signals of our volunteer. Your words can ensure correct interpretation.

Without understanding, guesswork may add error and confusion to the pain, and increase the emotional distance between you. We may think it's fine to protect others from our misery, with silence or denial, but this can backfire. Rather than feeling protected by your silence, friends and family may feel shut out, or cut off from your relationship. And, if they appear to accept your silence for extended periods, you may feel they don't care. These lies arise from our darkest emotions. Silence is not always golden.

TRUTH WINS OUT

Dishonesty also creates separation from others. It can weigh on us, growing to feel like a shameful secret and it can breed guilt. Shame, guilt, and separateness are not helpful in the pursuit of life, liberty, and happiness.

Unintentional small fibs may trip us more often than big lies. We recognize the "big whoppers" and can usually avoid them. But, is it a big deal if a friend asks how we're doing, and we answer, "Oh, just fine" when, in fact, we're suffering? Maybe it is. We may think we're protecting them, or perhaps our own fragile dignity. We may presume these little white lies are just part of a social ritual and don't mean anything. But, if you are going through depression, with no one to confide in, then the load you carry, in the role you are attempting to play, may get heavier with each performance.

Over time it can become a crushing weight, since the act has to be repeated so many times a day for weeks, months or years. Being free to open up about how you really feel, and what you are going through, can help build the support system you need. It can, and does, have a real impact on recovery. Burdens are lighter, when someone shares the load.

Jack Nicholson's character riveted our attention in the movie, *A Few Good Men*, as he thundered his famous line: "The truth? You can't handle the truth!"

You might suspect that also applies to your friends or family, and it might for some, but not all. If you're convinced that it does apply to all of them, then find a therapist or counselor, a pastor, a support/self-help group like the NAMI Connection mentioned earlier, or someone else you can trust, to listen to your truth.

We all need someone with whom we can openly talk about our needs, without worrying about disbelief, or judgment. Or concern that others will be either dismissive, or so afraid of what we say that they will instantly want to *fix* us.

A SERIOUS PERSONAL CHOICE

Deciding whether or not to reveal our issues, and with whom, is a critical, personal choice. There are no right or wrong answers about how many to tell, or whom those people should be. It may be scary to risk disclosure, but, in most cases, the benefits can far outweigh the risks. Risking disclosure, and sharing our hearts might lead to disappointment, but it could also lead to closer relationships, great support, and to hearing beautiful and healing words, such as, "I understand," or "I've been there."

If we share our hearts we can know the truth. When it comes to facing sadness or depression, we have all 'been there' at some time in our lives. Together we can help each other to be able to say, "I'm not alone—and I'm still standing!"

We don't need to be experts to make an amazing difference. Connection is more important than answers. If we're willing to reach out to others by asking for, or offering contact, we may save a life (our own—or someone else's), with simple words, just like the tourist-angel-man in our opening story. Who knows?

CONNECTION STRATEGIES

Some powerful connection strategies you can use:

- Pray: Ask God to make you increasingly aware of His presence, to guide you through this darkness and to strengthen you. Give thanks that you are never truly alone.

- Be inspired by others: Review, and try some of the coping strategies mentioned in our survivors' stories.

- Hold fast to your faith. Remind yourself that even when you can't feel His presence, God is with you. When you feel faithless—He is faithful. His strength is perfected (perfectly displayed) in our weakness. So, even if you're too weak to do anything but cry, when you trust and just hold on, you still provide a potentially spectacular display of God's grace. Good job, you're a witness!

- Review your favorite supportive scriptures, and your journal. Remember that God's words, in your voice, can unleash powerful healing.

- Be mindful. Stay in the moment. Avoid replays of past pain. And, no forecasting of *future* worries is allowed.

- Seek Joy and deliberately focus on the positives. Play the "glad" game. Do you recall the story of Pollyanna? When she wished for a doll, but received a pair of crutches instead, she immediately looked for something to be glad about. She focused on being 'glad' not sad, by giving thanks that she wasn't injured so she did not need to *use* the crutches, but could save them for possible future need. With this approach, you're setting or re-setting your brain's RAS attention thresholds to register the "good stuff."

- Paint, write, sing, dance, or work. Get busy with activity that lines up with your values. Savor (or find), a meaningful purpose.

- Find a way to lighten up with a bit of humor. Share laughter with someone whenever it's possible. Use jokes, movies, books, or other things to lighten your spirit.

MAKE PERSONAL, PHYSICAL CONTACT

Make sure that every day includes some personal, physical contact with another human being. It doesn't have to be intimate or prolonged. You can start with small, quick connections. Consider approaching just one person (stranger, family or friend), with a comment or observation on the day. This will help you. And you can't predict how much your simple words might mean to someone else.

CONFIDE YOUR STRUGGLE

Consider talking with your pastor, family member, or some-one close to confide your struggle. Ask for what you need. If you can't identify anyone you feel okay doing this with, consider calling a professional, or a consumer group. Call NAMI for referrals.

SCRIPTURE FOR MEDITATION

We are not meant to be isolated. We need each other. And, as we've already confirmed, we are never—not ever, truly alone.

"Neither height nor depth, nor anything else in all creation, will be able to separate us from the love of God that is in Christ Jesus our Lord." Romans 8:39

Pass it on!

CHAPTER 22—LONELY HEARTS & HIGH COSTS

D id you know loneliness is an international, multi-billion dollar issue?

The high cost of health care, and "Big Pharma" is not news for most of us. When we think of devastating health care costs we might picture major surgeries or medications, and long courses of complicated or exotic treatment. But, loneliness is one of the costliest concerns for health care.

In Great Britain, a recent report of the Jo Cox Commission on Loneliness estimated that it costs UK employers 2.5 billion pounds every year, which is 3.35 billion US dollars. They add that disconnection in and between communities may be costing their national economy 32 billion pounds (43.2 billion dollars) per year. It's a big enough concern to rate official representation in national and international businesses and governments.

Britain's Prime Minister, Theresa May, officially appointed a Minister of Loneliness, with the charge to assess and develop strategies to address it. Loneliness has grown from an intimate, personal issue—to an international problem. Crossing life's ages and stages, it affects us all, at some point. Getting lost in loneliness for any length of time is hazardous to our health. Loneliness is reportedly more dangerous than obesity, or smoking 15 cigarettes per day, and is reported to potentially shorten our lives by an estimated seven and a half years.

CareMore, (a subsidiary of Anthem, Inc., is a US health plan and delivery system. The AARP Bulletin (June 2018, page 42), cited CareMore's earnings of 1.2 billion dollar revenues, and reported this for-profit corporation has hired a Chief Togetherness Officer. The job is to address the issue of loneliness, and explore ways to mitigate its costs and impact on our health. Other enlightened agencies may soon be joining them. We can too.

For those suffering from major depression, social isolation and loneliness are familiar facts of life, as both symptom and cause. What can be done? Much! And, while we can appreciate, even cheer for, national and international efforts to recognize, define and assess the problems, and then to seek large-scale solutions or interventions, we don't have to wait for them. We can become "ministers" of our own wellbeing. In fact, to maximize progress with recovery from depression, we must.

How can we tackle such big issues when depression often has us feeling so inadequately small? We take baby steps, and we "keep on keeping on."

The stories of famous depression survivors provided some good strategies for living in the light. But, I often find myself wanting more than good advice. I want nitty-gritty details. How about you?

There may be some days when we can't even imagine finding a safe place to take our first shaky steps back into social connection. So let's start there with detailed, do-able practices to help you feel better, break isolation, and reconnect.

STRATEGIES

Here are practical strategies you can select from. Choose the ones that best meet your needs.

GIVE THANKS

In the morning, before your feet hit the floor,—pause to give thanks for being alive and being loved. Even in that first groggy moment when you're not sure how happy you should be about facing another day, and not necessarily *feeling* the love, the fact remains that you are here, and you *are* loved.

You have a God-given purpose to fulfill. You may not yet know what that will be, and maybe you're not thrilled about it right now, but each morning is a perfect opportunity to offer a sacrifice of praise. Try taking an inventory of things to be thankful for.

If you can't think of present things in your life to be thankful for, then try giving thanks for things that are absent. Do you have excruciating pain right now? If so, is it in every part of your body? No? Well, thank God! The "glad game" can be tough and it does take discipline, but it also offers great reward. Your "broken hallelujah" is a treasure.

Don't be afraid to 'tell it like it is' as you talk things over with God. He already knows your thoughts. Ask His help and guidance for the day. He hears every word. Even prayers that feel like they rise no higher than your ceiling can reach the throne of heaven. You are not alone. Start your day with that acknowledgment. It will help.

SEEK ORDER

Make your bed before you leave your room in the morning. Gretchen Rubin, the bestselling author, and researcher on the topic of happiness, said that making your bed was the number one, most meaningful change for increasing happiness that people have repeatedly described to her.

And then we have the word of a Navy Seal, William H. McCraven. In his 2014 commencement address, at the University of Texas, he told graduates they could start to change the world by making their bed every morning. He said accomplishing the first task of the day will spark a small sense of pride and will encourage doing another, and another. He advised that path would lead to success.

There are strong added benefits to this for people suffering from depression. By making this a habit, regardless of the way you feel, you are asserting control. This can relieve feelings of being helplessly *out* of control, and trapped by your emotions. You do have some power.

GET SOCIAL

A slow start at becoming socially active is fine. Baby steps are good. You could start by going to a coffee shop or drive-thru and just speaking to the person taking your order.

When this is comfortable, consider taking yourself on a solo date for lunch or dinner. Dress up. Make it a special treat. Speak to wait-staff as often as needed to place your order, and enjoy good service. Take pleasure in being around others even if you don't join them in conversation.

FEEL THE ENERGY OF A CROWD

Treat yourself to a sporting event and just enjoy sitting with a crowd of enthusiastic fans. You don't need to budget major league events. Try local high school or college sports.

ENJOY UPLIFTING MOVIES

Go watch a movie—or invite someone to watch one with you in a theater or on DVD. Aim for positive entertainment. Mysteries and adventure are fine—but, for this purpose, I suggest happy endings.

Comedy is best. As we have seen, laughter is good medicine. We have stacks of research to prove it.

ATTEND COMMUNITY EVENTS

Look at community newspapers or city magazines to find schedules of local events like concerts, pie eating contests, auto shows, rodeo, or anything else that appeals to you. Then, get out and enjoy one, by yourself, or with a friend.

LEARN SOMETHING NEW

Check your local Adult Education or Community College catalogue and sign up for a class you would enjoy. Learn some-thing new while you get out of the house and engage in as much (or as little) student interaction as you desire. Try painting, ceramics, guitar, drumming, photography, or one of many other possibilities. Caution: For classes that earn a grade, consider taking a credit/no-credit option if you have reason think you will be taking a more serious academic path in the future. Your goal is to enjoy this class without adding stress about grades.

MEET UP WITH LIKE-MINDED SOULS

The Internet can help with incredible sites such as meet-up.com. There are group meetings listed for a huge variety of interests, hobbies, jobs, and locations. You will find listings for quilters, skateboard artists, gourmet cooks, writers, crafts-people, master gardeners, and hundreds of others.

Take heart, the people you will meet at these gatherings share your interests, and your goal for social contact. Connections may be as tenuous, or as solid as you like. You can start slow and build over time. This resource, and others like it, is definitely worth checking out.

BECOME A VOLUNTEER

You can find opportunities for volunteer service in every area, and in a wide variety of needs from beach cleanup to mountain trail maintenance, wildlife rescue, shelters, literacy centers, food banks and more. Working to meet someone else's needs is a fabulous, effective antidote to isolation and loneliness. It's difficult to feel so helpless or hopeless when doing so.

These efforts offer rich, and satisfying rewards. Find opportunities by checking with local volunteer agencies in your area. Check community hospitals and relief agencies, or go on-line to check needs posted by causes you already know of, and care about. For example, to help others and get some exercise, you might contact Habitat For Humanity and volunteer to swing a hammer or help in some other way. Check them out (habitat.org/volunteer). The Salvation Army has many different kinds of volunteer positions open. Their web site addresses use the name of your town plus their organization designator (example: sacramento.salvationarmy.org). For more ideas, try an on-line search for volunteer opportunities. Thousands will be listed. You can find one to fit your interests and personal gifts, and to meet community needs.

RECREATIONAL READING

Lose yourself in a good book. When you take a recreational book *break*, avoid academic, how-to or self-help texts. Make it a gripping story that occupies your imagination for a while.

You can do this at home, but you can double the impact by getting out to your local library, or by finding a spot in a coffee house, where you are in the company of others.

TRIP OUT

Try taking a bus or a ferry ride to a random, pleasant destination. Play tourist in your own hometown. You could do more extensive traveling, but you can also benefit from short hops that offer a simple change of scene.

BECOME A DOCUMENTARIAN

A Stanford University study, completed in 2015 reported that a simple walk in nature or parklands for 30-90 minutes is enough to reduce the activity levels of the part of our brains that processes negative thoughts. So, why not get out and take pictures of beautiful public scenes. As long as you are in a public space—you may amplify social benefits by including people or pets you observe who are enjoying them. Document the happiness. Use your camera or smartphone. Aim for variety and interest.

Seeking beauty and joy, like a treasure hunt, can be helpful. It gives you a reason to get up, get out, and be among people. It occupies your mind with positive thoughts and documents your success. It sharpens your photography skills. It also activates brain systems that fine-tune our attention and help us break away from negative spirals, so we can more easily notice and enjoy the beauty or pleasure around us.

CALL A FRIEND

Social media is fun and can be very useful, but we need to make real-time sensory connections too. You could use a friend's post as a cue to call them instead of just replying on-line. Notice the suggestion is to *call*, not text. We want to hear their voice and actively use our own.

If you have the equipment, make it a visual (Skype or Face-Time) call. Seeing your friends and family, as you communicate, multiplies the joy and benefit. If you don't know how to do this, check into a local class, ask your neighbors' teen, or call your high school or college and ask if a student-mentor is available for a reasonable fee.

Caution: Don't let over-use of social media get you down. Making comparisons between your experience, and how great everyone else's life looks, can increase your dissatisfaction. Remember that what you see on social media is highly selective. We want to let the good times roll, while we appear in the best light possible. Very few people go public with their failures or post their sad/bad moments. Don't get caught in that trap.

JOURNAL

As you review your journal entries, do you notice increased understanding or coping skills? Be sure to give thanks to God, and to give yourself credit for your efforts.

Write a short description of your progress. What has been most helpful? What seems most meaningful for you right now? Celebrate achievements! Are there entries you would share with others who might experience some of the same struggles?

SCRIPTURES FOR MEDITATION

WE NEED EACH OTHER

- "Ointment and perfume delight the heart, And the sweetness of a man's friend gives delight by hearty counsel. Do not forsake your own friend or your father's friend, Nor go to your brother's house in the day of your calamity; Better is a neighbor nearby than a brother far away." Proverbs 27:9-10

- "Two are better than one, Because they have a good reward for their labor. For if they fall one will lift up his companion. But woe to him who is alone when he falls, For he has no one to help him up. Again, if two lie down together, they will keep warm; But how can one be warm alone?" Ecclesiastes 4:9-11

RELATING TO OUR STRATEGIES

- "Through the Lord's mercies we are not consumed, Because His compassions fail not. They are new every morning; Great is Your faithfulness." Lamentations 3:22-23

- "Therefore by Him let us continually offer the sacrifice of praise to God, that is, the fruit of our lips, giving thanks to His name. But do not forget to do good and to share, for with such sacrifices God is well pleased." Hebrews 13:15-16

- "O Lord, You have searched me and known me. You know my sitting down and my rising up; You understand my thought afar off. You comprehend my path and my lying down, And are acquainted with all my ways." Psalms 139:1-3

- "And let us not grow weary while doing good, for in due season we shall reap if we do not give up." Galatians 6:9

And finally, keep this one close to your heart, no matter what you feel you have or have not accomplished. It's unconditional.

"For I am persuaded that neither death nor life, nor angels, nor principalities nor powers, nor things to come, nor height nor depth,

nor any other created thing, shall be able to separate us from the love of God which is in Christ Jesus our Lord." (Romans 8:38-39)

Pass it on!

PART THREE:
BODY TALK

"Let's get physical!" Olivia Newton-John once made that idea a hit as she sang and danced across a movie screen. We are about to hit the final section of our study, and dancing is a reasonable suggestion.

Our thoughts, movements, and sensations, all travel the same wiring in neural pathways—sending and receiving commands and responses in our two-way traffic flow of impulses and signals. Understand this promise: Since all signals use the same wiring, we can stimulate, and strengthen those pathways by engaging in *any* of those activities.

Once a pathway is made through a jungle, regular traffic of any type (human, animal or mechanical), will maintain it. Take this analogy to inner space. All signal traffic uses the same pathways (or creates new ones). So, we can strengthen our thinking by moving— and we can strengthen our movement performance by *thinking*, as witnessed by athletes who use visualization, and by those times you were able to think more clearly or creatively when taking a walk

Knowing what we do now of the two-way neurological traffic between our bodies and our brains, it makes sense to learn all that we can about keeping both healthy and making the most of our bi-directional potential.

In this section, we will explore the body-blow impact of depression, and the powerful physical strategies for recovery that we can find in movement, diet, and sleep. It's a feast of learning and a dance of hope.

I pray that you will be inspired and encouraged as you discover more of the physical power you have, and how to use it. May God grant you peace, strength, comfort, and endurance for the journey.

"To this end I labor, struggling with all His energy, which so powerfully works in me." Colossians 1:29

CHAPTER 23 — A BREATH OF NEW LIFE

There is an incredible beauty and elegance to the living works of art that we are designed to be—all of us, not just the "super-model" few. Have you ever heard of someone being described as "poetry in motion?" That's us! We are God's living poems and works of art, and we're designed to be in motion.

Our lives are a love story filled with mystery, challenge, wonder, war and peace (both internal and external). It may play out, at times, as a tragedy, an inspirational epic, or a sidesplitting comedy.

Our production is staged on varied levels of mind and body integration. Only the top two levels are observable, our behaviors, and our performance style.

Other people may judge our public faces, but they can't see our physiology, internal communication, inspirations, or intentions. The greater part of who we are, and why we are—the *way* we are, is known only to our God and, to a lesser degree, ourselves.

LIFE-AFFIRMING SCIENCE

Dr. Alan Watkins, a neuroscientist, suggested that if we stacked life into a multi-level framework, a top-down view of our unique life operations would show these levels.

Level A: Observable—Public lives (Top Levels)

Performance: This is how well we act out the story of our lives—in public.

Behaviors: Things we do in our performance (polished or unpracticed).

Level B: Internal Conscious Lives. These are known to ourselves and to our God

Thinking: Our assessments, responses, and plans. These drive our behaviors (performance). Our thoughts respond to our feelings.

Feelings: The emotions we are aware of that shape and influence our thinking.

Level C: Hidden Internal Lives. These are known to God, but *not* always to ourselves

Raw emotions: Feedback from all systems is converted to energy signals entering the brain. This creates *raw* emotion we are often not aware of.

Physiology: Our brains and bodies are an integrated system, with sensory monitors checking operations at all times. Every second of every day, the business of living goes on—often below the level of our attention.

Why should we focus on streams of data about unconscious, automatic activity, when our goal is to discover and employ strategies to cope with, or control, our conscious states of mind? Because, all of the data streaming signals entering our brain are forms of energy. *Emotion is energy in motion.* That simple statement is profound. And because it's true, we have the ability to achieve the benefits of some conscious control, even over automatic body functions.

We are all in motion, all of the time. Our breath and heart beat are two prime and immediate examples. Both of these affect, and are affected by, our physical, mental, and emotional state. We can learn to take advantage of our two-way traffic flow, and our R.A.S. shifting abilities, to impact the entire framework of our lives. Motion conducts the flow.

COUNT THE WAYS

We monitor our health by-the-numbers when we check our weight, pulse rate, blood pressure, or oxygen saturation rate. Heart Rate Variability (HRV) is another measure well worth knowing. Much as we might enjoy 'jamming' with a good band, the most beautiful of all basic rhythms, our human heartbeat, needs certain regularity, not jazzy improvisation.

Imagine a quiet, deeply relaxing interlude suddenly, unexpectedly interrupted by a hot rendition of *"When The Saints Go Marching In"*... performed by a New Orleans Jazz group, who burst into the room, with full measures of volume and enthusiasm. If you were monitoring your heart at the very moment that jazz band blasted in, with its rocking, shocking performance, your heart rate would most definitely vary upwards from your resting state.

Your heart rate, displayed on a good monitor, would seem chaotic with the first rush of startled surprise. It would settle a bit as you recovered from the shock and enjoyed the energetic music. The regularity of heartbeats, called coherent rhythm, would eventually be restored, at a faster rate.

Speed and rhythm describe our heartbeats. The speed of heartbeat is measured in our pulse rate. Rhythm reflects the distance between the beats of your heart. These, vary over time, with or without a New Orleans Jazz Band. Heart Rate Variance (HRV) is a critical concept, as you shift from a steady state to chaos, and back to steady. We have no direct conscious control over increases in HRV. It is programmed for automatic responses to challenge or pressures, such as stress and/anxiety.

Did you know that chaotic signals entering the brain cause it to enter a stress response, effectively shutting off the function of your frontal lobe, shifting you to Level One operation? It's true. Dr. Watkins referred to this as a type of "Do-It-Yourself Lobotomy." Isn't that amazing. In times of chaos or great stress, just when we may want to be thinking most clearly—we may lose access to the executive function of our brains.

Stress, anxiety, and increased risk for depression thrive in chaos. We need coherence. The good news is that we are not helpless. We can invest in it.

EINSTEIN ON PROBLEM SOLVING

Albert Einstein said that the same kind of thinking used to conceive or create a problem—cannot be used to solve it. He said if we want to resolve problems, we must change the context of thoughts that conceived them. We can build on that advice. We can change our *physical* context to move from chaos to calm.

When the imaginary jazz band appeared, your heart rate probably would have zoomed from a resting rate of 60-70 beats per minute (bpm), to 140-160 or more bpm. HRV chaos would reign, caused by the startle effect, before your heart settled back into a regular, but faster, rate of 80-120 bpm. The drop in rate would depend on how quickly you adjusted, and whether or not you were content to just listen, or if you got up and danced.

Your normal respiration rate would also probably change dramatically. You might gasp in chaos. That gasp would be an involuntary response, and a very large clue to a rapid change in your physicality. Have you ever had moments of breathless anticipation?

A NOTE ABOUT ANGER AND FEAR

Jazz bands may be the most fun, but they aren't the only things to get our pulses stirring and to shake things up within us. Fear and Anger are undisputed champions in that arena. Imagine being put on *'hold'* by an emergency nurse, whom you called to ask if your sudden symptoms could signal a heart attack.

Fear ? Yes √

Frustration, leading to anger? Yes √

As understandable as those emotions are, they could set up a near perfect storm of incredible chaos for your poor heart to endure, in *addition* to whatever the first set of difficulties may have been. You must *choose* to calm the storm as much as possible.

Here's the point, your breath may change as an involuntary automatic response to experience, but you can also *consciously control* your breathing. In doing so, your physical "context" can change quickly, and you can rapidly move from chaos to more coherence. For everything except a heart attack or other medical emergency, prove this to yourself with a basic breathing exercise. (For the heart attack—hang-up and dial 911!)

STRATEGIES

PRACTICE RHYTHMIC BREATHING

You can practice deep rhythmic breathing anytime, and anywhere. It's a completely portable, ever-ready tool you can use to control chaos, reduce stress, improve your ability to think clearly, and enhance your mood. It belongs to you free of charge, and is completely within your power to control.

Think of the rhythm of ocean waves flowing in and out, at regular intervals. Establish a rhythm of deep breathing. You're breathing deeply when air fills your lungs and pushes on your diaphragm, so that your tummy moves out.

Breathe to a regular count. Try inhaling through your nose to a slow mental count of four, and then exhale as if gently blowing out a candle, as you slowly count to six. Change the count a bit, if needed. Consistency and comfort are the keys. With practice you can maintain rhythmic breathing and change your HRV, from chaos to coherence, often within one minute.

IMPORTANT DETAILS

While you are breathing to your comfortable and consistent count, focus on a smooth flow of air. Not a choppy stream, but like calm ocean waves, with smooth ebb and flow. Breath control is not something to fear as associated with some alien practice. Mentally focus on what blesses you as you breathe.

POINT TO PONDER

By a classic dictionary definition, to "inspire" means to inhale, taking in life-giving oxygen. And to "expire" means to exhale, clearing carbon dioxide from the lungs. Believers can find enriched meaning in breathing exercises. The Holy Spirit *inspires* us. As we acknowledge His presence, we are able to breathe in joy and exhale our confusion and pain.

Focus on the physical sensations of your breath expanding and filling your chest. With that intake, also take in a deep realization of God's presence and love for you. Feel it. Then, as you exhale, let your stress or difficult thoughts be released along with the used air and gases you are letting go. Thus, rhythmic breathing becomes a spiritual experience. Use this exercise, and focus, to find coherence and peace again. Do it as often as needed.

BREATH PRAYERS: AN ACT OF PRAISE

Try matching a prayer to the rhythmic count of your breathing exercise. For example, slowly inhale through your nose while silently praying, "Thank you Jesus." Then, slowly exhale in time with silently saying, "I'm letting go right now."

Notice the number of syllables match the 4/6 rhythm for inhalation and exhalation as recommended for exercise. Feel free to make up your own one-breath-prayers to keep your rhythm and your focus ideal. We can feel our hearts swell with incoming Grace, as we are "inspired," and relax with the "expiration" of stress we don't need to carry.

JOURNAL YOUR JOURNEY

What are you discovering? How can you use your discoveries for maximum benefit?

SCRIPTURES FOR MEDITATION

"And the Lord God formed man of the dust of the ground, and breathed into his nostrils the breath of life; and man became a living being." Genesis 2:7

"Let everything that has breath praise the Lord" Psalm 150:6

CHAPTER 24—GOING WITH THE FLOW

We have more choice and power over our own well-being than we might suspect. As we learned, thousands of potential new brain cells are born every day. They must be fed, connected, and protected. Brain chemistry is the vital flow that automatically helps with all of that.

Signals that regulate our physical functions at every level, also power our thoughts, dreams, memories, and imagination. These sparks are relayed through billions of connections, over the many miles of wiring within our neural networks.

Toxic levels of stress break down the connections between these billions of nerve cells. Depression and Anxiety disorders are linked with toxic stress.

In addition to eroding vital neural connections, studies have also shown chronic depression may contribute to shrinking certain brain areas. Where neural connections break, we lose the signal transmissions and/or coordination, which determines if we will live, as well as what quality of life we will enjoy.

We may not be surprised by the impact of disruptions in our amazingly complex and delicate design. But, the simplicity of one of our most powerful remedies *is* surprising.

At our lowest and weakest point, when all we have are tattered scraps of hope, we are not helpless. We can choose to move, and in doing so, we may go on, beyond a frozen, broken state, into positive *action* that helps us move into rehabilitation.

NAMI (The National Alliance on Mental Illness (NAMI) reports, "Studies have shown that exercise can reduce anxiety and depression and improve mood, self-esteem and cognitive function." (info@ nami.org)

Here's why that's true. Movement can trigger a cascade of brain chemicals and growth factors capable of shifting moods which stops the damage of chronic stress and depression, and can even reverse the process. With our movements, we can actually direct the supplies, the availability, and the use of our own fabulous brain chemistry.

In their book, *Spark: The Revolutionary New Science Of Exercise and The Brain*, doctors John Ratey, and Eric Hagerman introduce research showing that physical activity actually 'sparks' changes within the brain that encourage neurons to bind to one another.

Movement and physical activity are broad terms. With so many benefits to gain, we may ask:

- What kind of movement packs this kind of brainpower?

- Are different moves needed for different issues?

- How should I do it? Will I be able to learn what I need to know?

- What equipment, or strength will I need?

- How much movement is required?

- Is there a specific schedule to follow (Time, Duration, Intensity)?

- What about physical limitations?

- Will it hurt? What if I have no energy?

We might also wonder if something so simple can offer any real relief for depression or anxiety? The answer is yes!

THE SCIENCE OF PHYSICAL MOVEMENT

Thanks to our two-way traffic design, the same network pathways used to sense and signal movement, are used for transmission of other sensations and for our thoughts. Strengthen these pathways with either, and you enhance both physical and mental abilities. Skilled movement can also serve as an on-ramp to traffic flow within specific locations of the neural network. It can provide access to blocked or damaged areas, allowing for re-connection, expansion, or even development of new pathways in major work sites of the brain.

Understanding the logic, and mechanics of movement (exercise) strategies can help to prop up our, sometimes sagging, motivation, as can the assurance that it works.

Is movement the magic cure for depression? No. But strong evidence reveals these benefits among others:

- Effective relief of symptoms

- Reduction in severity and duration of depressive episodes

- Improved ability to cope with difficulty

- Increased hope

- The ability to feel some control over our circumstances

- Enhanced quality of life.

WILL IT REQUIRE EFFORT?

Yes. Can you do it? Yes, you can—and you're worth it!

As impossible as it may seem, our divine designs allows us to be active participants in the maintenance and recovery of our own physical and mental health. We can even adjust our un-conscious, automatic systems (to our benefit) by our choices and actions. Movement changes brain chemistry. It shifts stress and depression, and may help to reverse it. Of course, check with your doctor before starting new exercises.

Be encouraged. Our divine designer is a God of love and power. He wants to share His love and power with us. These verses will encourage you.

Speaking of the restoration of a city, and of His people, God said: *"Behold, I will bring it health and healing; I will heal them and reveal to them the abundance of peace and truth."* Jeremiah 33:6

Added assurance: "But Jesus looked at them and said to them, *'With men this is impossible, but with God all things are possible.'"* Matthew 19:26

Action within each brain-cell is electrical. Each impulse is a spark. When enough sparks hit a neuron, reaching its response threshold, it 'fires' to send its signal on. These sparks of brilliance cause chemical releases, moving us in the flow of life.

Some neurotransmitters stimulate brain cells to fire—and others calm things down. We recognize Adrenaline, and Cortisol (linked with 'action', alerts, or stress), as well as Dopamine and Serotonin (famous for calming, and 'feeling -good').

HOW TO TRIGGER YOUR BRAIN CELLS

We can stimulate a flood of excitable chemistry using just our imaginations. We need the inhibiting ability of others to keep us in balance, and to disrupt the flow of negative feedback that can sweep us away.

Brain chemistry explains what's behind certain strategies we can learn. It adds confidence, and intention to our use of them. As amazing and complex as our chemistry is, with thousands of automatic actions and reactions, it is equally amazing that our divine design also provides a manual over-ride. We can use exercise to shift into manual control.

Physical movement reduces the resting tension of our muscles. This interrupts the feedback loop of anxiety to the brain. This is the "Worry Loop" Dr. Hallowell wrote of in his book. He suggests that we can break out of obsessive worry loops by immediately engaging in movement at the first sign of trouble. Something as simple as standing up and beginning to sway—can break the negative feedback.

I love that suggestion, and have en-joyed its benefits. I invite you to *SWAY* with me: **S**top **W**orrying **A**bout **Y**ourself.

THE SCIENCE OF SWAY

The rhythmic, gentle movement of swaying (rocking, swinging, or gliding) has a calming effect. Calm bodies aren't as likely to worry or remain stuck in an anxious, depressive spiral. There is a science to how this works. Let's explore it.

1. Gently exercising immediately upon arising increases levels of norepinephrine in parts of the brain. That wakes us up and

gets us going with a kick-start to attention and motivation, while improving mood and giving us a sense of control.

2. Regular long-term exercise increases dopamine storage in the brain, and supports the creation of receptors in the reward center of the brain. It increases the level of endorphins in our system. These natural pain relievers also contribute to our feeling good.

3. As muscles begin to work they use fat molecules as fuel. The process of converting fat into fuel also frees tryptophan to enter the blood stream. Tryptophan is the building block for Serotonin. With exercise, blood levels of this chemical get higher and more concentrated.

To restore balance in the blood flow, tryptophan pushes through a barrier and enters the brain. Once inside, it is immediately used to manufacture Serotonin. To be used inside the brain, Serotonin must be produced within it. Exercise makes this happen.

Do lower levels of Serotonin contribute to depression or does depression cause decreased Serotonin levels? The answer may be *both*. There is no question about the importance of adequate Serotonin levels. Exercise starts the manufacture of Serotonin in the brain.

4. Neurotransmitters do the signaling between brain cells in the neural network. The network itself needs constant rebuilding and maintenance. A different family of chemicals is required to accomplish this, and to monitor signal traffic. Dr. Ratey described one of these chemicals (BDNF) as Miracle-Grow for the brain.

BDNF is the short name for Brain-Derived Neurotropic Factor. It encourages growth, strengthens and improves the function of neurons, and protects them against cell death. It is critical for directing signal traffic, and engineering the paths themselves, within

212

the neural network. It is a physical link between thoughts, emotions, and movement. Exercise increases levels of BDNF.

5. A different neurotransmitter, Gamma-amino-butyric acid (GABA), is the brain's major inhibitor. It works like brake fluid, helping to interrupt obsessive feedback, which we have called a worry loop.

GABA is the target for many, if not most, anti-anxiety medications. We need a balanced supply. We need enough, but not too much of it. Without enough GABA, neurons fire too easily and too often, stimulating the negative feedback-back loop in the brain. With too *much* GABA you may feel that you can't get moving. Research suggests depressed and bipolar patients tend to have lower levels of GABA in their blood.

Balance is important. So, if you find GABA supplements on the market, use them only with your health professional's guidance. Medication is not a good Do-It-Yourself project. But you *can* do something good, on your own. Physical activity triggers a natural, balanced release of GABA in the body.

6. Atrial Natriuretic Peptide (ANP) is a less well-known chemical agent. It's very important but, perhaps, under-appreciated. Let's take a close look at it in the light of one of our instinctual sparks of brilliance.

"Fight—Flight—or Freeze" is a reflex response to extreme stress. We know how it feels. Physical symptoms include increased heart rate, and spikes in blood pressure. These are part of the high costs of maintaining stress over time. There is some good news.

Our God's designs are amazing. As He so often does, He gives us the power to deliberately affect how it all works. We can't control our physical responses to stress. They're automatic reflexes. But we *can* deliberately shift from automatic to manual control when we notice them. This is powerful damage control we can do for ourselves, because God, our divine designer, gave us that power. How? We can choose to move.

When our hearts start beating hard, muscle cells produce this defensive chemical. We can intentionally raise our heart rates with safe levels of exercise. Increased heart rate causes increased production of ANP, which gives the body another tool for putting the brakes on our stress response.

Physical activity is a key to helping us to "go with the flow" and to assure that the flow (of brain chemistry itself) is non-toxic. Choosing to move is critical, it's powerful, and it's within our control.

When we feel at our weakest, and our energy reserves fall to near zero, we may tell ourselves that exercise is completely beyond us and that what we need is rest. That's not true. Those sad, exhausted times are the moments of critical choice, and *exactly* when we need to get up and do something.

STRATEGIES & SMOOTH MOVES

Science has proved that motion reduces stress and depression. So, we want to prioritize adding more movement. *Motion creates emotion.*

ASK FOR AWARENESS

Talk these things over with the Lord. Ask Him to help you see and recognize the points most important to you. Ask for His wisdom to guide you, and for His strength to give you power for living—right now.

TRACK YOUR ACTIONS

Keep track of your level of activity in your journal. For two weeks, commit to making a note of the amount of time you sit or sleep and the amount of time you are active. See if your moods keep up with your energy and activities.

TAKE BABY STEPS

In your very next moment of despair—ask for help, give thanks, and *choose to move*. Start small, maybe just a walk to your front door where you open it for some fresh air, and a look at the world outside. Build up to walking around the block, and move on from there. Remember that old proverb… a journey of a thousand miles begins with a single step. Take baby steps.

SCRIPTURE FOR MEDITATION

"He gives strength to the weary and increases the power of the weak. Even youths grow tired and weary, and young men stumble and fall; but those who hope in the Lord will renew their strength. They will soar on wings like eagles; they will run and not grow weary, they will walk and not be faint." Isaiah 40:29-31

A prayer for you as we leave this chapter:

"Beloved, I pray that you may prosper in all things and be in health, just as your soul prospers." 3 John 1: 2

CHAPTER 25 — MOVING MOUNTAINS

Prescribed medication, and natural chemistry triggered by exercise, are both powerful. Both may be needed, along with other tools or strategies, to cope with major depression or anxiety. There is nothing wrong with combing techniques.

"Every good and perfect gift is from above, coming down from the Father of the heavenly lights, who does not change like shifting shadows." James 1:17

Prescribed medication must be prescribed, and used under the care of your doctor. Exercise is a treatment you can prescribe for yourself. Of course, if you have any physical health concerns, be sure to check with your doctor before beginning an exercise program. You are in charge of filling the exercise prescription, at no additional charge, and with no negative side effects when used wisely.

NATURAL CHEMISTRY

The American Journal of Psychiatry published "A Call to Action: Overcoming Anxiety through Active Coping." In this article, neuroscientists Joseph LeDoux and Jack Gorman described a strategy for linking new pathways in the brain, and shifting signal streams away from the negative threatening messages, which can snowball into an avalanche of anxiety and troubling emotion.

Muscle tension sends feedback to the brain, which can heighten anxiety. This happens unconsciously in response to stress, anxiety, and depression. The good news is that if we engage in immediate physical exercise at the first conscious sign of anxiety, we can re-route a fear-based information stream away from emotional processing centers of the brain to, and through, our brain/body motor circuits instead. Exercise reduces muscle tension, and that interrupts the negative feedback loop from body to brain.

When we are stressed, our brains recognize increased heart rate and faster, shallow breathing as symptoms of anxiety or panic, which can spiral out of control. But these are also *normal* responses to aerobic exercise.

We can apply healthy aerobic activity to match the symptoms—linking faster heartbeat and breathing to beneficial out-comes, rather than the panic our brains may have been expecting. We can break the cycle, and take advantage of the chemistry we reviewed in the last chapter.

The absence of motivation is at the heart of depression. But we can retrain the brain. We can redirect negative signals with exercise. Brain training through exercise works for depression as well as anxiety. When your body moves, your brain must also move. Engage!

Staff at Duke University conducted a study in 1999 titled, "Standard Medical Intervention and Long-term Exercise (SMILE)." In this work, Dr. J. Blumenthal, et.al, reported that for every 50 minutes of weekly aerobic type exercise, participants showed a 50% percent improvement in their scores on a common test of depression.

They also found walking or jogging at a pace that meets 70-85 percent of individual aerobic capacity for 30 minutes, three times per week resulted in improvements that equaled those gained from certain antidepressant medications.

A 2006 study by Dr. M. Triveldi, Director of Mood Disorders Research Program at the University of Texas Southwestern Medical School, found that patients, who did not find relief with medication, were able to enjoy a 61% percent improvement in scores on a common test of depression, after 12-weeks of prescribed exercise. An impressive amount of research supports the benefits, and prescribes exercise for the relief of depression and anxiety. Three major questions arise:

1. What kind of exercise is best to release natural chemistry?

2. How much exercise and how often?

3. How long before we see results?

Let's start finding answers with a look at some obvious truth:

- Physical Activity is any type of body movement for any period of time.

- Any movement is better than no movement at all.

- Exercise is defined as a prescribed routine, for a specified period of time.

- The best exercise is the one you will actually *do*.

- Consistency is the key to success.

- Check with your doctor before beginning any new exercise routine.

Now, we'll focus on our questions:

1. What type of exercise seems most effective?

High doses of prescribed aerobic exercise gained the most (50-

60%) percentage of improvement, but even low-intensity exercise is beneficial.

Don't let a busy schedule, or lack of energy keep you from physical activity. A 10-minute walk has been shown as effective as a 45-minute workout for a temporary lift of depression's moody blues. The effects of such a short, one-time, activity will be temporary, and can't offer the full lifting power of regular exercise, but it's still useful, in the same way that taking aspirin is helpful for temporary relief of a headache.

2. How much exercise is required? How often?

A long-standing, general recommendation is that we exercise for a minimum of 30 minutes, three times per week. That's not bad advice, but research suggests we can get much more personal and specific than that. You can calculate your personal requirements with an evidence-based prescription for treating your depression with exercise. Here's how to do that.

- High Dose. To find the number of calories you need to burn per week for the greatest benefit, multiply eight calories, per each pound of body weight. For example, if you weigh two hundred pounds, multiply by eight calories (200 x 8 = 1600). This is your target for a weekly calorie burn.

Now, divide this sum by the number of workout sessions you plan per week. If you work out five times per week, you'll need to burn 320 calories per session. Working out three times per week requires burning 533 calories per session. Check your gym's equipment tracker or use other references to learn how many minutes you need on a given activity to reach the required calorie burn.

- Low Dose. Use the same calculation methods—but substitute three calories instead of eight, per pound of body weight, as your multiplier.

Aerobic exercise is any exercise that raises the heart rate, increases respiration, and allows you to sustain it. This is the gold standard. Other, non-aerobic, physical activities have also been found helpful for coping with, or lifting, depression and anxiety. For example, Stretching, Yoga, Tai Chi, and meditation have all been studied, and each shown to offer some benefit.

Let me stress that using the physical movements or strategies of Yoga, or Tai Chi does not require us to dabble in foreign religions. We must simply keep the spiritual focus of our activity on the Holy Spirit. When we do, all prayerful meditations will be addressed to our loving, living God and upon His truths.

Regarding a believer's use of worldly knowledge, techniques or products—we have a model in scripture.

"So then, about eating food sacrificed to idols: We know that an idol is nothing at all in the world, and that 'There is no other God but one.' For even if there are so-called gods, whether in heaven or earth (as there are many 'gods' and many 'lords'), yet for us there is but *one* God, the Father, of whom are all things, and we for Him; and one Lord, Jesus Christ, through whom are all things and through whom we live." 1 Corinthians 8:4-13

This verse illustrates the freedom we have. When we know that the Holy Spirit reigns, and that our hearts are for the Lord, we are free to partake, (decently and in order,) of whatever is good that the world has to offer for our own benefit, and to God's glory. We need to be sensitive about the faith of others. Not everyone shares the same understanding and level of freedom. Be careful, to avoid wounding other believers.

STRATEGIES

Here are some techniques that will help you make the first move and keep going.

MAKE GOD YOUR MOTIVATOR

Talk things over with God. Share your thoughts with Him and ask what He thinks is good for you. Give thanks for understanding, for life, and for love.

START BY STANDING UP

Once you're up, *do* something! Jog, walk, bike, dance or try some other aerobic fun. Do this three to five times a week for 30 minutes at a time.

BE CONSISTENT, NOT PERFECT

Aim for consistency rather than perfection. It's better to walk every day for 15-20 minutes than to wait until the weekend for a fitness marathon. Frequency and consistency are most important.

BABY STEPS

Set small, achievable daily goals. Acknowledge and reward your efforts.

ENJOY MOVEMENT YOUR WAY

Find activities that are fun or enjoyable. You might try classes, or go solo.

SPICE UP YOUR EXERCISE TIMES

Download music, audiobooks, or podcasts to accompany your workout. Music offers the power of rhythm to keep you going, and listening to things you enjoy offers distraction so you don't get bored. Consider creating a Contemporary Christian or Gospel music playlist for your workout. If you build one, please feel free to share!

GET SOCIAL

Try the buddy system. Being accountable and supporting a friend makes it easier to stay on track. Encouragement from a buddy can be a big boost.

BE PATIENT WITH YOURSELF

We might see some immediate short-term improvement. Long-term change will take more time. Most people need about four to eight weeks before they feel natural and coordinated with a new exercise routine. As you get in better shape, exercise will feel easier.

How bad do you feel in your worst or weakest moments? Use that answer as a measure of how badly you need exercise. Words of encouragement: Research assures us that even folks who hate exercise have a definite and positive mood upswing the minute their workout is over. That's quick relief!

SCRIPTURE FOR MEDITATION

"Now may the God of hope fill you with all joy and peace in believing, that you may abound in hope by the power of the Holy Spirit." Romans 15:13

CHAPTER 26—FINDING YOUR SWEET SPOT

C rouching there, in the dark, shivers chased down my spine. *"They're so close. I can hear footsteps and whispers. They must not find me."*

In desperation, I ran to hide as fast as I could, out-running even my breath. Trying not to gasp, or make any sound at all, I clapped my hand over my mouth to suppress… the giggles.

*   *   *

As I remember it, playing hide and seek, was fun. I also loved singing, bicycle rides, running for the sheer joy of it, climbing, swinging, sliding, bouncing, twirling, dancing, and swimming on hot summer afternoons. Those summer games were best when followed by picnics and ice-cold watermelon slices. What fun do you remember? When was the last time you experienced that joy?

Albert Einstein once likened life to riding a bicycle because, in both, to keep your balance, you must keep moving. He also said, *"Play is the highest form of research."*

Let's do some research. Can you describe your own play style? Check the following sampler against your preferences:

PREFERRED ACTIVITY STYLE

- Cycling: Solo or in a group? Leisure or racing? Off-road or on?

- Swimming: Laps or splashing around? Water Polo or Water Aerobics?

- Basketball: Shooting baskets or a full game? For fun or competition?

- Dancing: Solo or line-dance? Square dance, Salsa or Ballroom? Other?

- Frisbee: Solo or playing catch with a friend or pet?

- Walking: Leisure or Power Walk? Groups or solo? Hike or race?

- Skiing: Snow or water? Solo or team? Fun or Olympic training?

Notice your patterns. Do you crave vigorous physical activity or do you prefer a slower, more relaxed pace? Do you like competitive or cooperative play? Do you want solitude or more social contact? Do you prefer activity outdoors or in-doors? Write down your answers. They will be helpful to you.

Stroll down memory lane. What childhood play activities did you most enjoy? Can you do them now? If it was "kid stuff," can you think of a way to update it for adulthood? If not, can you just give yourself permission to enjoy it anyway, especially now that you have very grown-up, scientific reasons for it?

If the play you used to enjoy is now beyond your physical abilities, is there a way to adapt it? Can you identify what you enjoyed most about that activity? Can you find those things in another resource? Does bowling have to be downtown or could a Wii game, X-Box, or other format work for you?

If it's expensive, can you reduce or share expenses? Can you find a lower cost alternative with at least some of the important characteristics you need, or could you just *do it* as an investment in your own health and enjoyment?

THE SCIENCE OF FITNESS AND FUN

Calculate your personal, prescription-strength dose of exercise for the relief of depression and anxiety. Aim to hit these targets in play, as well as more routine activities. Fitness and fun are fabulous, and even more so when they are combined.

Here are a few examples, based on research from the official journal of the American College of Sports Medicine (*Medicine and Science, in Sports and Exercise*). Burn rates are reported as calories-per-hour, in minimum to maximum range depending upon body mass (130-205 lbs.), intensity, duration of activity, and other variables:

ACTIVITY AND BURN RATES

- Cycling: Burns 236 to 1489 calories per hour (depending on BMI, pace, terrain, and intensity). Is it a casual ride or the Tour de France?

- Swimming: Burns 236-931 depending body mass, pace and style, (treading water—or swimming rapid freestyle laps).

- Basketball: Shooting baskets burns 266-419. Playing a competitive game can burn 472-745.

- Dancing: Dance burns 177-512+ depending on pace, and style. Rock on!

- Frisbee: Solo targets, casual play, or a game of Ultimate? There is a wide range from 177-745.

- Walking: Burns 118-745 depending on body mass, equipment, speed, and terrain.

- Gardening: Burns 236-372, depending on the intensity of your labor.

This very incomplete list does not include hundreds of other games and activities you might think of. Have you tried Pickle Ball? How about kite flying or fishing?

Formal programs, classes or routines, with or without a gym membership and exercise equipment, were not included. If you have a gym membership, ask what fun forms of exercise they offer.

The most difficult challenge we face is not likely to be in finding enjoyable activities. It is in facing the fact of our depression, recognizing our need, and then getting up to do something, in spite of it. The moment you feel at your worst is when you most *need* to move!

Paul wrote about working out our faith.

"For it is God who works in you to will and to act in order to fulfill His good purpose." Philippians 2:13

I believe this applies to our spiritual as well as physical and mental lives. When motivation needs a boost it may be especially helpful to remember that gifts are given with the intention that they will be used. We have been given fabulous bodies, as well as minds. Let's use them.

What if you can't find the *fun* in activity? Do it anyway. At the very least you will see yourself acting on your own behalf—in spite of your misery. As you enjoy the powerful feelings of control in choosing to move, and as movement sparks improvement, the fun may get easier to find.

Remember to give yourself credit for every small step you take. Write it down. You are building a body of evidence that progress is possible. Use that encouragement the next time you find it hard to get yourself going.

If the term "couch potato" feels like the right description for your current activity level, don't waste time or energy on self-blame. There is no condemnation, just choose today to start moving and keep doing it.

Remember Newton's Law? He proposed that bodies in motion tend to stay in motion—and that bodies at rest tend to stay at rest, unless acted upon by another force. We have access to the greatest Force, and it isn't science fiction. I pray we will allow the Holy Spirit to move us through the dark—toward health and recovery.

STRATEGIES

It's one thing to get in motion, and another to keep in motion. These strategies will help you do both. May *the* 'Force' be…

PRAY FOR MOTIVATION

Ask God to give you the strength to get up, get out, and do whatever you can to move in your own behalf. Give thanks for all that you have to be grateful for, including your first breath this morning, physical, financial, or relational blessings, sunrise, the absence of pain in some part of your body, and the many other things that will come to your mind.

REMEMBER YOUR FORMULA

Set your goal. Seek variety to burn your ideal amount of calories per week. Aerobic activity is the gold standard, but all movement is good. It's even better when seasoned with a bit of fun, friends, and laughter.

DISCOVER ACTIVITIES NEAR YOU

Most communities have some kind of directory of activities from their parks and recreation departments. Check these out for ideas and inspiration. Searching on-line will expand your idea file. What will you look for?

MAKE EXERCISE SOCIAL

Looking for an exercise buddy, or play pal? Post a note on your church bulletin board, or community center. Work and play with friends is highly recommended.

Remember this verse: "Two are better than one, because they have a good return for their labor: If either of them falls down, one can help the other up." (Ecclesiastes 4: 9-10)

JOURNAL YOUR EXERCISE JOURNEY

Write what you learn about yourself and your capacity for enjoyment. Give yourself credit for your engagement. Track your progress, energy levels, and moods. Note any improvements or discoveries.

SCRIPTURE FOR MEDITATION

Paul explained a life of faith in our God, when he said, "For in him we live and move and have our being. As some of your own poets have said, We are his offspring." (Acts 17:28).

CHAPTER 27—FOOD FOR THOUGHT

Is mental health on your menu? If not, it should be. We have all probably heard, "We are—what we eat." New research shows that we think and feel what we eat too. Diet is just as important to mental health as it is to physical health.

Considering all that we know of our divine design, the integration of every system in our bodies, and the importance of chemistry to every spark of life throughout the brain/body system, we should not be shocked by the idea that food and drink play important roles in mental health. Our personal chemistry includes everything we put into our bodies as well as everything the body manufactures.

It's been suggested that we could be healthier and happier if we relied more on "FARMacy" rather than the Pharmacy. Dr. Mark Hyman, a New York Times best selling author, and medical director of the Ultra Wellness Center, describes food as the medicine that is more powerful than anything else he has in his tool kit to prevent, treat, and even reverse disease.

Is the FARMacy idea more than a half-baked theory? Yes. According to an all-star cast of world-renowned doctors, researchers, and nutritionists, it's one of the most important ideas that we all need to understand, and act upon.

Do your eyes glaze; your mind fog, and your emotions go into revolt as you think about diet and nutrition, because of different and conflicting ideas? Most of us have many questions about dieting. For example:

- Is high protein, low carb a good balance?

- Do calories count?

- Which is best, Paleo or Vegan, or should we try something in between?

- Does fat make us fat? Should we avoid it or do we need it? Is there such a thing as good fat? We know the brain is 60% fat, and look what all *it* does for us!

Let's get some answers to these and many other related questions.

BRAIN SCIENCE ABOUT EATING

Important studies show direct links between the quality of diet, and mental health. Dr. Daniel Amen, a board-certified psychiatrist and neuroscientist, has said that "brain envy" is one of the factors that moved him to focus on food. Having scanned thousands of brains in his work, he knows what a healthy brain looks like. He wanted his brain to be as beautifully healthy as the best he had seen. He shared a startling observation: As our weight goes up—the size of our brain goes down. I did not know that. Did you?

As we launch into this topic keep these truths in mind:

- Depression knocks us off balance physically and mentally

- Imbalances in the body show up in the brain.

- We are what we eat. It seems that we think and feel what we eat too.

There are three main dietary threats to our physical and mental health:

1. Nutritional Difficulties

2. Immune and Inflammatory Imbalances

3. Digestive Imbalances

We're going to explore these and identify strategies to cope with them. There is great hope in this exploration.

Nutritional Deficiencies are caused by:

- Not eating enough of the right stuff;

- Not getting the full value of nutrients in the fruits and vegetables we choose because of the way they're farmed, processed, or transported;

- Not being able to digest and absorb the "good stuff" from what we do eat.

Let's look at each of these.

THE RIGHT STUFF

For good health, our bodies' need: carbohydrates, vitamins, proteins, fats, minerals, and water. Our Divine Designer God put these together in a variety of delicious foods. He loves us. He did not design our taste buds and create chocolate to torture us. Instead, He offers a feast of flavors for us to enjoy, including chocolate. We just have to be wise to thrive, choosing the right foods in the right amounts.

Carbohydrates were listed first in the food elements we need. So, let's shine some light on that great debate.

To carb or not to carb, that has been a question. The scientific answer is, "Yes." We must eat carbs, because all cells and tissues need them. They are the body's biggest source of fuel, and they're needed for intestinal health.

All carbs are not equal. There is a difference between simple and complex carbs. Our fearful and wonderful human design is complex. Our ideal carbohydrates are too. If we thought of nutrition as a sport, the real Super Bowl could be a salad! Ideally, fruits and vegetables would fill 50-75% percent of our plates. Expert advice tells us to "eat the rainbow." The more intense and varied the colors of the foods we eat, the richer they are in content and variety of the nutrients they offer.

Complex Carbs are most often found in whole foods, and they contain fiber as well as other nutrients. These are loaded with benefits. Complex carbs are digested slowly in a sustained release of energy, so your hunger may feel satisfied longer.

Simple Carbs can be thought of as empty. They add sugar, but very little (or no) fiber or other nutrients. These break down fast in digestion offering a rush of energy followed by the familiar "crash" as they are consumed by the body in a hurry.

They can affect the brain in ways similar to drugs of abuse. Did you know some studies show sugar is as addictive as cocaine? It's true. Simple carbs cause or worsen low moods by creating spikes in blood sugar, which are followed by a crash. This roller coaster may look like fun, but it's not a healthy ride.

These foods should raise a red flag:

• Candy

- Colas (and other sweetened drinks)

- Pastries

- Refined white bread and pasta,

- White Rice.

My brilliant granddaughter summed up saying, "If it's white, take flight," I agree, with the possible exception of dairy products.

Dairy is a different form of simple carbohydrate. It does not have fiber, and it does add sugar, but it is not empty of nutritional value, as simple carbs so often are. Dairy offers vitamins, calcium, proteins, and fats. Yogurt, with active cultures, also helps maintain the balance of healthy bacteria in the digestive system.

You may have reasons to avoid dairy products, but they are not pure dietary villains. If you have difficulty with complex carbs, such as gluten sensitivity or food allergies, adjust selection as needed, but don't avoid them completely. As always, when in doubt, check things out with your healthcare specialist or nutritionist.

Let's get back to complex carbohydrates, the unquestionable "good guys." We find them in fruits, vegetables, and healthy grains. Complex carbs, along with the other food elements we listed, play a major role in the onset, severity, and treatment of depression and other mental health issues.

THE ABC'S OF COMPLEX CARBOHYDRATES

This is a short list of some good sources:

Asparagus, Amaranth, Bananas, Blueberries, Black Beans, Cantaloupe, Cucumber, Fruits (wide variety), Kale, Millet, Pears,

235

Peas, Pinto Beans, Papaya, Quinoa, Spinach, Strawberries, Sweet Potatoes, a variety of other vegetables, and Whole Grains (barley, bulgur, oats, wild rice).

This list is not complete—it's a sampler, meant to whet your appetite for more information. There are many great resources for more information. I hope you will check them out on-line or in your local library.

Complex carbohydrates are a source of many needed vitamins, minerals, and fiber. Folic acid is one of the B-Vitamins, and it's of special concern to us because of its importance for the production of Serotonin, Dopamine, and Norepinephrine. Did you know a deficiency of folic acid might be a major cause of depression and mood disorders? In fact, depressive symptoms are the most common neuropsychiatric symptoms of Folate deficiency. B-Vitamins can't be stored in our bodies, and our bodies cannot manufacture Folate. We can get what we need only in our diets, or with supplements.

We all understand the need for fiber in our diets, right? Complex carbohydrates are champions of the menu because they meet both of these needs, for B-Vitamins and for fiber. Let's take a closer look at some of these all-stars.

MOST VALUABLE PLAYERS

One cup of pinto beans yields 74% percent of the needed daily value of folic acid, plus other important vitamins and a significant amount fiber. Asparagus is another winner. Eating four spears of asparagus provides 22% percent of this needed daily value.

Popeye may have put spinach on the map, but you don't need to be a sailor-man to benefit from it. Leafy greens such as spinach, romaine, turnip and mustard greens, are all high in folic acid and other beneficial nutrients. Beets and lentils are also good sources.

Broccoli is a good source of folic acid and Selenium, which is important for our immune and reproduction systems as well as thyroid metabolism. Special note: low levels of Selenium may contribute to depression, anxiety, and fatigue. Other sources include chicken, onions, seafood, walnuts, Brazil nuts, and whole-grain products.

Bananas are high in potassium, protein, and fiber. One medium sized banana contains about six percent of the recommended daily value of folic acid. By the way, oatmeal has also been cited as having a positive effect on easing depression. Could we easily combine these two? Yes! This seems like a great time to suggest diet combinations, for flavor and for healthy favor. Let your culinary imagination play with ideas. Combine ingredients and multiply powerful benefits.

In a 1958 musical comedy, *Auntie Mame* the main character sang, about life as being "just a bowl of cherries." A decade later, comedy writer, Erma Bombeck, asked, "If life is a bowl of cherries, what am I doing in the pits?" I've occasionally wondered about that myself, and you may have too. Could it be that we admired Mame's theory but failed to *eat* the cherries?

Cherries are a wonderful source of Vitamin C, Vitamin A, Calcium, Protein and Iron. And, because they are a good source of Melatonin, Cherries have been suggested to aid sleep. They are reported to help with other concerns too, but cherries are sweet. Be cautious of the amount of sugar you consume in them.

Berries offer important nutrients, and they contain polyphenols, which give them their deep red or blue colors. Polyphenols activate proteins that clean up damaged cells, breaking down and recycling toxic chemicals. Enjoy them in all varieties including Blueberries, Blackberries, Strawberries, Boysenberries, Raspberries, Acai Berries, and others. Fresh picked is fabulous, but frozen varieties are equally effective.

Researchers suggest berries may also significantly reduce the risk of depression, heart disease, stroke, cancer, high blood pressure, constipation, allergies, asthma and diabetes. How much would you pay for these health benefits? These are truly "'berried treasure."

PROTEINS ON PARADE

Proteins are another important nutrient we must have. Lean proteins are made of amino acids, which are the building blocks for life. One of these amino acids is tryptophan, which produces Serotonin, nature's Prozac. Only eight of 20 essential amino acids are made in the body. The others must come from diet.

Find lean protein in fish, turkey, chicken, eggs and beans. Note that there are also good plant sources for protein. If you are vegetarian, check with your nutritionist to be sure you get all essential acids.

Combinations are critical. Lean protein is the source for tryptophan production, but complex carbs are required to help tryptophan enter the brain to reduce symptoms of depression and anxiety.

FAT: FORBIDDEN, OR FABULOUS?

"Fat is not a 4-letter word." So says Dr. Mark Hyman. Our bodies need fat for physical and mental health, and (surprise) even for weight loss. But we need the right *kind* of fats—in whole foods, in healthy proportions and in the right combinations. If we mix fat with too much processed, highly refined foods, and add lots of sugar, then we not only lose the benefits—but we may create a time bomb of future health risks.

S.A.D. is the acronym for our Standard American Diet, and it *is* sad in the effects it may have on our health. A very low-fat diet is not a universal answer. It may even work against us. Our brains are made of 60% percent fat. One third of that is in the Omega-3 family. The body can't manufacture this. We must get it from our diet. Foods rich in Omega-3 include wild cold-water fish, like salmon, herring, sardines, and mackerel, as well as seaweed, flaxseed and walnuts.

Other mono-unsaturated fats also benefit brain and body. Find these in things like olive oil, avocados, coconut, egg yolks, and butter. An imbalance in the ratio of Omega-6 and Omega-3 fatty acids may contribute to depressive symptoms. So, we need to increase healthy Omega-3's, reduce industrial oils, and avoid trans-fats completely. Think of traditional deep fryers and Twinkies as potential hazards.

H^2O: *Oh!*

Water is life to us, and it's a key to our quality of life as well. Dehydration, even as little as 10 percent, may result in decreased cognition, increased confusion, stress, and anxiety. Dehydration may also contribute to depression. At the very least consume six to eight full glasses of pure and refreshing water daily.

STRATEGIES

We have looked at a wide variety of foods that can help us live happier lives. We have seen why their contribution is important. Here are strategies for striking balance.

MAKE GRACE A PART OF YOUR PROCESS

Thank God for the delicious variety of food, and ask for the protection and cleansing He provides. Pray for wisdom and strength as you review your eating habits and make plans for improvement.

Recognize that all calories are not equal. It's much more than simple math so choose wisely. Likewise, all carbohydrates are not equal. They are not all villains. We need complex carbs for life, and we want them in combinations.

Some fats are fabulous and are required for healthy, delicious diets. Did I mention that our brains are 60% percent fat? Now, that's a fabulous fact.

RESEARCH AND RECORD YOUR FOOD CHOICES

Your journal can help you track your emotions. Research shows that we can experience sadness as hunger. When we do, eating healthy fat instead of salty or sugary snacks can reduce cravings. Note your responses in your journal for future reference. The same goes for other food choices. Document them.

- Try some avocado, a hard-boiled egg, or a handful of nuts for a healthy snack.

- Be cautious with the balance of your sugar intake. Avoid chemical artificial sweeteners and limit simple carbohydrates.

- Try eating several small meals throughout the day. Stop eating three or four hours before bedtime.

- Think of fruits and vegetables as your new fast food favorites. Keep them on hand, ready-to-go, for instant gratification, and for long-term benefit.

- Water is essential. One suggestion even recommended that we consume a number of ounces of water, equal to one-half of our body weight, daily. For example: 192 lbs. = 96 ounces of water. That's equal to three 32 oz. bottles of water per day.

- For foolproof selection, here is a bit of advice from experts on the subject: If food grows on a plant, it's good to eat. If it's manufactured *in* a plant, then consider better possible choices.

- Cooking can alter the nutritional value of our fruits and vegetables. Raw is almost always a great choice. I've been told that frozen foods are also great.

- Good resources on this topic exist and are not hard to find. Do an Internet search, and prepare to be amazed.

SCRIPTURE FOR MEDITATION

"Every moving thing that lives shall be food for you. I have given you all things, even as the green herbs." Genesis 9:3

"So, whether you eat or drink or whatever you do, do it all for the glory of God." 1 Corinthians 10:30

CHAPTER 28 — COOKING UP RELIEF

W e identified immune and inflammatory imbalance as the second major dietary risk to our physical and mental health. But what does this really mean?

Inflammation is actually a part of our immune response. It is the body's means of self-protection—part of the attempt to remove harmful irritants, and to start the healing process. We need this response. It's only a problem when things get out of balance. It's easy to spot the fever and external swelling of inflamed responses to a cut or injury. It's harder to recognize the inside stories.

Research shows there are links between depression and internal inflammation. When it's out of balance—it is out of control.

Trouble often starts in our diets, when we get more than we bargained for in the farming and processing of foods we eat. Concerns may be added accidentally or on purpose, such as: genetic modification of seeds, pesticides, the richness or depletion of soil, harvesting methods, and delays or difficulties with transportation from farm-to-market-to-table. For meat products, we can add concern about the use of hormones and antibiotics. All could negatively affect nutrition, digestion and inflammation. What's a person to do?

Courage! We're not helpless or hopeless. We have blessings to count and choices we can make to brighten this picture and safeguard our mental and physical health.

EATING CLEAN

The US Department of Agriculture certifies food as "Organic" if it's produced with no synthetic chemicals, fertilizers, genetic engineering, radiation or sewage sludge.

Organic fresh fruits and vegetables, (and grass-fed or wild-caught meats and fish), are what I think of as a 'clean' diet. Yes, I know that labels can be confusing, and costs may be a bit higher, but there are budget-minded choices we can make, and it's worth thinking about.

The good news is that not every fruit or vegetable carries equal risk. The Environmental Working Group is a good resource for information and 'risk' ratings of fruits and vegetables. Those with lower risk for pesticides and genetic engineering, are called the "Clean Fifteen." They call the higher risk choices the "Dirty Dozen." Here's an abbreviated summary.

THE CLEAN FIFTEEN

Avocado, sweet corn, pineapples, cabbage, frozen sweet peas, onions, asparagus, mangos, papaya, kiwi, eggplant, grapefruit, cantaloupe, cauliflower, and sweet potatoes.

THE DIRTY DOZEN

Apples, peaches, nectarines, strawberries, grapes, celery, spinach, sweet bell peppers, cucumbers, cherry tomatoes, snap peas, potatoes, hot peppers, kale, and collard greens.

Some of my favorites are listed in the Dirty Dozen. Perhaps some of yours are too. Don't worry we still have some good options. We can buy the Clean Fifteen from traditional bargain sources and, if the budget allows, select our favorites of the Dirty Dozen, from organic sources. Problem solved!

If the budget won't stretch for organic sources on some of our favorites, just use more care in cleaning and preparation. Health experts say eating conventionally grown produce is far better than skipping fruits and vegetables. So, don't eliminate these foods, just give them a good cleaning. They offer important nutrients and delicious flavor to our menu for good health.

A WORD ABOUT VITAMINS AND MINERALS

Vitamin deficiency has been strongly linked to depression, anxiety, and to risks for physical health. Research reports special concern for Vitamins B1, B6, B12, C, and D. Vitamins are best found in the clean, fresh, rainbow of foods we can choose.

Minerals are important for healthy function and balance of physical and mental status. Two all-stars, Magnesium and Zinc, can serve as examples. Magnesium has been described as the ultimate "chill pill" because it helps balance hormones and is needed for release and re-uptake of Serotonin.

Zinc helps transcribe proteins and create neurotransmitters. Heavy metals can damage or destroy brain cells. Proteins work overtime to clear the metals we are exposed to in our polluted world. The heavy workload may cause depletion of Zinc.

Our food is not the same as it was a hundred years ago. We all may need a good, daily multi-vitamin in addition to a healthy diet. But radical supplementation is not a great Do-It-Yourself project. We could miss something or get too much of a good thing, which may be equally undesirable. Seek guidance. If you decide to use supplements, be sure to read labels and "When in doubt—Check things out" with your nutrition or health specialist.

SUGAR AND SPICE AND EVERYTHING NICE… REALLY?

In 2014, the United States Department of Agriculture (USDA) reported that we each ate, (on average,) 150 to 170 pounds of refined sugars per year. That's astounding.

Well, we are all sweethearts, but is that much sweetness good for our hearts? According to a crowd of doctors and other health specialists, the answer is a resounding "No." The Mayo clinic reports refined sugar is the principal driver of Type 2 Diabetes and Heart Disease.

In his book, *The Sugar Solution*, Mark Hyman, M.D. says that regular sugar intake leads to inflammation, high blood pressure, increased risk of cancer, and depression. To illustrate the effect of sugar on the brain, he suggests picturing the crunchy, golden crust on a good Crème Brule. Sugar reacts with proteins to form plaques that make our brains "crusty." Also, sugar consumes the body's store of vitamins and minerals—without giving a nutritional return. Sodas and fruit juices, as well as processed baked goods and refined starches are some of the biggest sources of our trouble.

We need to be cautious about sugar. In one of its many guises, it may be a hidden ingredient in processed food. We need to read labels carefully, and to remember that sugar, by any other name, can be dangerous. Have you "Googled" the 56 other common names for sugar yet? It's an adventure in label reading.

WHAT ABOUT SPICES?

Spices offer thousands of healthy phytonutrients, antioxidants and loads of flavor to our cooking—all with zero calories! They can add other benefits too. Some examples:

- Curry Powder includes turmeric, which contains curcumin, a powerful anti-inflammatory described as fifty times more potent than Vitamin C or Vitamin E.

- Oregano: One teaspoon has six micrograms of bone-building Vitamin K, and the same amount of antioxidants as three cups of spinach.

- Cinnamon: Antioxidant compounds in this spice help prevent spikes and dips in blood sugar levels. Eating half a teaspoon of cinnamon daily may reduce risk factors for diabetes and heart disease. (Add it to Oatmeal. Be creative!)

- Ginger: Elements in Ginger may reduce inflammation and block nerve pathways that process pain. Try thin slices of Ginger, (about 1 inch of organic root,) in a cup of boiling water (to make Ginger Tea) for headache relief.

- Nutmeg is rich in protective anti-inflammatory elements and antibacterial compounds.

- Cumin offers 22% percent of our daily requirement for iron, in one tablespoon. This supports energy levels and our immune systems. It might boost brainpower too.

- Chili Powder: Just a pinch can add flavor and offer Vitamins A and C, plus potassium, calcium, and even folic acid.

If this isn't spicy enough, an on-line search reveals at least 20 more beneficial spices.

Other foods recommended to help reduce inflammation risk include: Olive oil, tomatoes, nuts (like walnuts and almonds), leafy greens, salmon and mackerel, fruit (including blueberries and oranges). These are examples—but certainly not the only good choices.

STRATEGIES

Eating right takes some positive reinforcement for most of us. Here are some helpful strategies.

THANK GOD FOR THE FOOD WE HAVE

Thank God for the bounty of delicious foods He designed to support our physical and mental health. Ask for wisdom and strength to make wise choices. Consider our tradition of saying "Grace" before meals. It's so much more than just a ritual. It's an act of praise, and can offer protection.

In Acts 10: 14-15 we learn of Peter's vision, where God chose to use food selection to illustrate a profound lesson about acceptance. Peter was invited to eat non-Kosher foods. He responded: "Not so, Lord! For I have never eaten anything common or unclean." He heard a sure reply: "What God has cleansed, you must not call common." As we give thanks, we can ask Him to cleanse our food and bless it to our bodies.

KEEP TRACK OF WHAT YOU EAT

As you experiment with foods and spices, make a note in your journal of what works for you. Of course, avoid those things you believe are wrong for you. Track noted changes in your energy or moods. Be bold in your combinations. Be fearless trying new things. You might start a whole new journal just for recipes and experiments you enjoy in the kitchen.

ADDED TIPS & TRICKS

Try some of these "best practices" and food choices. Record your personal responses in your journal.

- Read Labels. Look for hidden additives. If you can't pronounce the words or understand what something is, it might be something to avoid. Ask questions.

- Eat Well. Check the suggestions listed in the last several pages and enjoy!

- Coffee Lovers:

Rather than reaching for the sugar bowl to fix your favorite brew, try one of these sweet ideas instead:

1. Cinnamon adds a touch of sweetness and offers an immune boost.

2. Coconut Milk, Coconut Cream: A healthy way to sweeten your coffee. Are you a latte lover? Try frothing these before adding to your coffee. Top it off with cinnamon. Enjoy rich, creamy flavor and sweetness-free from less healthful options.

3. Unsweetened Cocoa or Cocoa Powder. Chocolate can highlight subtle flavors of coffee beans, and add antioxidants too.

4. Vanilla or Almond Extract: Just a couple of drops may kill the craving for added sugar or sweeteners.

5. Avoid artificial chemical sweeteners. Seek natural alternatives.

SCRIPTURES FOR MEDITATION

"Oh taste and see that the Lord is good. Blessed is the man who trusts in him." Psalms 34:8

"But food does not commend us to God; for neither if we eat are we the better, nor if we do not eat are we the worse." 1 Corinthians 8:8

"For every creature of God is good, and nothing is to be refused if it is received with thanksgiving; for it is sanctified by the word of God and prayer." 1 Tim. 4:4

"Now may he who supplies seed to the sower, and bread for food, supply and multiply the seed you have sown and increase the fruits of your righteousness." 2 Corinthians 9:10

CHAPTER 29 — IS DEPRESSION A 'GUT' FEELING?

Amazing as it seems, , the answer is yes, it may be. Your digestive system can affect your emotional state in many ways. Depression has been called an inflammatory disease. In addition to nutrition and inflammation, the third and final dietary threat we will review is digestion. Of course, diet and digestion are not the only cause of depression or the only answer to relieving it. But these factors are extremely important.

In his book, *Brain Maker*, Dr. Perlmutter explains that not only is there a connection between the body and brain—but, if your tummy is in a bad mood, your mind is too.

Neurotransmitters are signal carriers, which open and close gateways of emotions. They influence our thoughts and memories, and direct our body functions. These 'brain chemicals', or their raw ingredients, are produced in the digestive system. Digestive bacteria also regulate the absorption and availability of these chemicals to the brain.

For at least a decade, antidepressants have been the number one prescribed drug class in the USA. I am not opposed to the use of medications. If needed, praise God they're available. Follow your doctor's advice. Be aware that medications don't treat depression; they only treat the *symptoms* of depression. The search for underlying causes is personal, and continuing. Meanwhile, we do well to also consider taking full advantage of the "FARMacy".

The answers to some probable causes (and relief) of depression and anxiety may be found in our own bellies. This means they are closer and more within our control than we may have imagined.

THE BELLY-BRAIN CONNECTION

Neural pathways of inner space handle all of our two-way signal traffic. This information flow controls our thinking, feeling and our automatic actions, in response to what's happening within our bodies, our lives, and our world.

Our nervous system handles this ocean of information. It's an elegant, multi-level system with two major distinctions, The Central Nervous system (CNS), and the Peripheral Nervous System (PNS).

The CNS includes the brain and spinal column. Information is checked and decisions are made here. The PNS includes sensory nerves and organs that monitor every condition of the body, inside and out, and sends information back to "Central."

Subdivisions of the PNS are designed for special operations. The Autonomic Nervous System (ANS) is the part of the PNS that takes care of the body's repeated automatic needs, such as breathing, blinking, and heartbeat.

This special ANS division is organized in three parts including: the Sympathetic; the Para-sympathetic and the Enteric nervous systems.

Stay with me here—I promise this will be worth knowing about.

The Sympathetic and Para-sympathetic systems work together to start and stop things without our needing to think about everything. If our body were a Lamborghini or Ferrari, the Sympathetic system would be our accelerator, and the Para-sympathetic system would be the brakes.

The Enteric Nervous system was discovered (about 60 years ago) within the layers of tissue forming the gastrointestinal (GI) tract. This system has more nerve cells than the spinal cord—100 million of them! It has been called our "second brain" because of its size and importance.

Scientists first thought these neurons all received information sent from the brain to the stomach. Newer studies show the reverse is true. It's now believed that 90 percent of these neurons are sending information to the brain from the stomach instead.

The strength and tight fit of junctures of the stomach lining prevent unfriendly contents from leaking directly into the bloodstream. If digestive by-products slipped into the bloodstream, they might penetrate the protective barrier of the brain, exposing us to illnesses and affecting brain function. This could also affect how well our medications work. A healthy digestive tract, with strong and tight junctures in the lining, has much to do with our happiness and general physical health. We want to keep it fit.

Disease, inflammation, infection, poor quality (or "dirty") foods, and physical injuries can cause things to go wrong. These are the villains. There are good guys in our story too. And sometimes the good guys can also get us into trouble. It's complicated.

For example, antibiotics can be heroes—as they wage war against disease, killing off bad bugs (infections). But wiping out bad bugs also kills off good bacteria. "Good" stomach bacteria are critical for digestion. It's needed for absorbing the nutrients required for physical health, and for producing those neurotransmitters needed for healthy brain functions.

When a war ends, reconstruction is needed. How do we rebuild? By making wise choices in the food we eat, with an emphasis on growing and supporting good bacteria. We're talking about basics like fruits, vegetables, good proteins, fiber, and good fats. We also need probiotics and prebiotics.

Probiotics and prebiotics may be listed last, but they are among the first in importance. Probiotics are friendly living bacteria, which support critical flora living in our digestive tracts. Prebiotics are non-living ingredients in food, which feed the good bacteria and help them grow. We need both for good digestion. Depending on your current condition and choices—you could see significant improvement in your micro-biome within six days. How's that for good news!

STRATEGIES

Proper nutrition is essential for health. We know that as it relates to weight or energy, but we often forget how important it is to our brain health and emotional wellbeing. Here are some strategies that could bring real benefits.

- Support your GI tract's garden of healthy flora. Find probiotics in fermented foods like live-cultured yogurt, kefir, tempeh, Kim chi, sauerkraut, pickles, un-pasteurized pickled fruits and vegetables (pickled in brine, not vinegar), and in fermented meats, like corned beef. Kombucha tea, hard-boiled eggs, and other foods may also fit on this menu.

- Some of the best sources of prebiotics are whole, natural foods including raw garlic, raw leeks, raw asparagus, cabbage, artichokes, certain grains, and both raw and cooked onions.

- Supplements may be useful to support rebuilding and maintaining a healthy and happy micro-biome. There are hundreds, if not thousands, of supplement formulas on the market. Read labels carefully. As always, check with your health care or nutrition specialist to be sure you get what your body needs.

- A REPEAT CAUTION: If you are using medications, are pregnant, or have any existing physical health concerns, be sure to share your plans with your doctor before making any big changes in your diet or supplementation

SCRIPTURES FOR MEDITATION

Prayers for you:

"Beloved, I pray that you may prosper in all things and be in health, just as your soul prospers." 3 John 2

I pray also that you will be blessed with fruit of a different kind: "...But the fruit of the Spirit is love, joy, peace, longsuffering, kindness, goodness, faithfulness, gentleness, self-control. Against such there is no law. " Galatians 5:21-23

CHAPTER 30 — SWEET DREAMS

Comedian W.C. Fields once said getting a lot of sleep would be the best cure for insomnia. He said it with a straight-faced, tongue-in-cheek delivery intended as humor. In spite of his legendary comedic talents, sleep loss is no laughing matter.

Visible signs of depression don't always include sadness, tears, and obvious misery. In fact, exhaustion and numbness are among the earliest recognizable symptoms.

Most of us have experienced not getting enough sleep, at one time or another. But, did you know approximately 70 million Americans of all ages suffer from chronic sleep problems? That's a big number, and a *huge* problem.

According to the Diagnostic Statistical Manual (5th Edition), one hallmark of depression is an upset in balance, either getting too much, or not enough sleep. Balance is essential. Excessive sleeping may be a short-term escape strategy, but it's not a good long-term solution. Lack of sleep can be miserable, and even dangerous.

Without sleep, our cerebral cortex may shift from monitoring at a Level 3 "ready state" to more of a Level 1 "high risk" status, causing increased subconscious levels of anxiety, repeatedly disturbing sleep. Sleep deprivation is a double-edged sword. It increases the risk of developing depression, and it may deepen depression for those already suffering its effects.

When asked his secret for success, billionaire, businessman, and investor T. Boone Pickens advised that we should sleep, and work for eight hours each, and be sure they are not the same hours. His witty 'secret' focused on our day jobs. But we want nighttime success too.

SLEEP SCIENCE

Sleep is our "time out," so we get to turn everything off and rest, right? Wrong! Sleep is an *active* event. It's not like clocking out at work and having time off. It's more like shift-change, and the night shift may be equally as busy as the day. Dr. Miller, a neuroscientist at The National Institute of Health, explains that during sleep, our bodies release hormones that help to repair cells and control the body's use of energy.

The night shift (in sleep) is the only time that some critical jobs can be accomplished. In waking, our brains receive thousands of stimuli per second from our auditory, visual, and neuro-sensory systems. The brain works hard just to keep up well enough to allow our day-to-day operations. But the brain can't possibly get all of this input sorted, evaluated and filed for long-term use, or discarded, during the busy day. So, the night shift has a heavy workload.

NETWORK DIVERSIONS

Just as traffic is diverted for major road repair, we need 'network' diversions too. The brain can't be busy handling signals in an uninterrupted flow of rush hour traffic and still be available for repairs, new construction or expansion of neural networks at the same time.

Old Testament wisdom tells us: "It is vain for you to rise up early, To sit up late, To eat the bread of sorrows; For so He gives His beloved sleep." Psalm 127:2

All of our learning, logical evaluation, planning, and decision making takes place during wakefulness, but the re-wiring needed to make those results permanent happens while we sleep. Loss of just one or two hours of sleep leaves us operating on a much different level from those who get the 7-8 hours per night needed for most adults.

A good night's sleep includes 4 to 5 sleep cycles, with periods of deep sleep, and periods of Rapid Eye Movement (REM) sleep. A complete cycle takes about 90 minutes.

Each stage in the cycle is important for the different types of work that must be done. For example, we may process and record procedural memory in REM sleep, and build declarative memory in slow-wave Non-REM sleep. There may be differences in processing emotions of memory in varied stages of sleep as well.

Our ability to communicate is also seriously impaired by chronic lack of sleep. Hearing and Auditory processing are critical for receptive language ability. Making sense of the information we hear, or adjusting to the amplified sounds of a hearing aid, requires new permanent wiring changes. These are done as we sleep. Expressive language (the ability to form and send coherent messages) also relies on brain operations that can be maintained only with sufficient quality and quantity of sleep.

VALID REASONS FOR VALUING SLEEP

- Sleep affects nearly every cell in our bodies—including those of our immune and cardiovascular systems, our appetite, breathing, and blood pressure.

- Lack of sleep may even reduce the efficacy of vaccinations.

- Sleep loss impairs higher levels of reasoning, of problem-solving, and attention to detail. Accident risks soar when we are sleep deprived.

- Over time, a sleep deficit can put you at greater risk for depression—and can make things worse, if you already have it. A vicious cycle of cause/effect may begin. We need to break the cycle.

- Sleep seems to be as important to our brain's physical health as drinking or eating is to our bodies.

- Sleep is important to brain development and it affects neuroplasticity in brains of all ages. It may also play a role in the maintenance and modification of brain cells' firing rates and sequences.

- Extended wakefulness can injure neurons essential for alertness and cognition.

Without enough sleep, neurons can begin to deteriorate, potentially causing both brain damage, and shrinkage. Trying to play catch-up on week-ends is not a good substitute. It doesn't work.

- Sleep helps restore the brain by flushing out toxins that build up during waking hours. Research at Rochester Medical Center recently found that toxic waste is removed during sleep through the Glymphatic system, which moves cerebro-spinal fluid through the brain along a series of channels. Experiments have shown that channel space increased by 60 percent during sleep, which improves flushing ability. The flow rate is reduced during our waking state as Glial cells (which form the channels,) swell with activity.

- Lack of sleep is linked to obesity. There is a circadian clock protein that regulates hormones, which play an important role in the safe accumulation of body fat. Fat accumulation leads to chronic internal inflammation, which contributes to diabetes and heart disease.

The most common sleep disorders are insomnia and sleep apnea.

For me, a simple change in routine, like an important meeting I need to be up early and alert for, can invite insomnia. My self-talk often goes like this:

"... I need to get up early and be sharp in the morning. Okay, I can get 8 hours of sleep if I start right now." I glance at the clock, and anticipate the meeting. "Oh dear, it's getting late. I must get to sleep." I glance at the clock again. "I can still get 6 hours... 4 hours... 3 hours... Why aren't I asleep yet?? Aaaarrrggghhh !" Can you relate?

SPIRITUAL RESOURCES TO AID SLEEP

King David's response to racing thoughts and threats are helpful. His self-talk is a great model: "I will both lie down in peace, and sleep; For You alone, O Lord, make me dwell in safety." (Psalms 4:8)

If the Psalmist could trust God when his enemies were on the prowl and planned to kill him, how much more reasonable it seems to let God handle my concerns. Hmmm, it's a good point. Maybe I can just say a prayer, and take one slow, deep breath, then another... and another... and... zzzzz.

CAUTION

Prayer and meditation are powerful sleep aids. Deep breathing helps too. Unfortunately, many of us are tempted to rush for aids of another kind. Sleeping pills can have serious consequences. Nearly 9 million Americans take prescription sleeping pills, and even more of us use drugstore remedies. Emergency room visits involving sleep aids doubled between 2005 and 2010. A majority of emergencies are related to sleep aids used in combination with other medications or substances.

Other risks exist. Some sleeping pills have ingredients that suppress REM sleep and dreaming, and have been linked to increased dementia in seniors.

I'm not advocating abstinence of medication. If it's needed, then thank God it's available, but please note that regular use of drugs such as sleep aids should not be a solo project. Take recurring sleep problems seriously and get checked out. Talk with your doctor or health-care provider.

RED FLAG WARNING

Sleep Apnea is dangerous. It describes a lack of air exchange for ten or more seconds at a time. Severity is measured by how many disruptions occur per hour. Obstructive Sleep Apnea is considered moderate with 15-30 disruptions per hour. Higher rates increase a variety of serious health risks.

According to a sleep study at Northwestern University, the body's fight or flight response is activated as oxygen levels go down. Blood pressure jumps, heart rate fluctuates, and the brain must partially wake you up, to start your breathing again. Not only do you wake with fatigue, moodiness, and impaired intellectual function, but apnea also affects the vessels that lead to the brain, so the risk of stroke is higher too. When in doubt, get checked out.

BLESSINGS

What a divine design we have! Isn't it just like our God to take care of so many critical operations for us during sleep when there is nothing we need, or can, consciously do to achieve them? When we sleep we stop striving, and we are blessed. We must allow time for sufficient sleep; give our concerns to God, and then just surrender to rest, while the night shift goes to work.

SLEEP STRATEGIES

Sleep disturbance can stem from everything from bad habits to serious medical conditions. Here are some sleep-related strategies to consider.

- Thank God for the blessings of rest and ask for His help to enjoy it. Talk things over with Him and meditate on His Word and promises.

- Get outside. We need 30-60 minutes of exposure to sunlight each day to adjust our circadian rhythms. The best time is in the morning or at noon. If your winter location doesn't provide that much sunshine consider using light-therapy. Ask your doctor for details.

- Get regular exercise, and do it several hours before bedtime.

- Go to bed at the same time every night, even weekends.

- If you suspect sleep apnea, tell your doctor and get an evaluation. Indicators are if you snore chronically or wake up choking or gasping for air, or if you chronically feel fatigued and sleepy during the day. Serious sleep apnea may require the use of a medical device to provide Continuous Positive Airway Pressure (CPAP). These are available by prescription. Don't hesitate to use it if you need this support. CPAP units can offer life saving, or certainly life enhancing benefits. There are several different style and size options. If you are reluctant to use such a device because of discomfort or irritation, check with your doctor about alternatives. Don't give up.

DIY TIPS FOR BREATHING EASIER

For less severe needs, non-medical intervention may help. To maintain an open airway while sleeping you may try:

1. Adhesive strips that open your sinus passages. Wear them during sleep.

2. Jaw or Chin straps can help keep your mouth closed and jaw in a forward position, which helps prevent the tongue and soft tissue from slipping backwards and, potentially blocking air-flow, as they relax. Try more than one style or size to find what's most comfortable and effective. You might need to seek professional advice, or to try more than one style or size to find what's most comfortable, and effective, for you.

3. Mouth (or teeth) guards protect against grinding. They can also help maintain open airways. Be ready to seek advice and to experiment a bit if needed.

OTHER STRATEGIES

For insomnia, try creating a nightly ritual for going to bed. You could:

a) Dim the house lights wherever possible, a few hours before bedtime. This may help with your body's change of rhythm.

b) Avoid alcohol within three or four hours of bedtime. Also, avoid stimulants like caffeine, within the same period.

c) Melatonin is a natural hormone regulator of the sleep cycle. Production may slow as we age, and is sensitive to other factors such as light exposure and temperature. Try lowering the temperature in your bedroom to prompt increased natural release of melatonin. The National Institutes of Health (NIH) suggest setting thermostats at 66 and 68 degrees Fahrenheit.

d) If possible, stop watching TV or using your computing devices 90 minutes before sleep. The blue light emitted by such electronics has been known to interfere with the body's responses and circadian rhythms, so that melatonin is not released as needed for sleep. If you must continue exposure to these devices, consider wearing Blue-Blocker glasses or getting a screen filter. Blue-light blocking glasses are widely available. I ordered mine on-line for less than 20.00 per pair.

e) Try having a snack 1 hour before bed. Yes, warm milk might be a good idea depending on your diet needs, but fresh cheese (not aged) and crackers can be even more effective. The protein and carbs help with tryptophan production (which has a beneficial effect on brain chemistry).

f) Relax in a warm bath or hot shower 30 minutes before bedtime.

g) Try wearing non-elastic, warm and comfy socks in bed. Cold feet can disrupt deep sleep.

h) Mask irritating sounds with "white-noise" such as the sound of a fan running, set so it does not blow directly on you. You could also try apps or devices offering sounds of nature, rain, waves, or soothing instrumental music.

i) Practice deep breathing exercises that you have learned.

j) Read, or write in your journal a few minutes before bed. Reflect on the blessings of the day and let God have your concerns.

These are just a few highlights of what is known about sleep. Many excellent books have been written on this subject. Check them out. Our final encouraging words are from the very best book ever written on any subject, the Holy Bible:

SCRIPTURES FOR MEDITATION

These verses are excellent for bedtime meditations.

"And He said, 'My Presence will go with you, and I will give you rest." Exodus 33:14

"Be anxious for nothing, but in everything by prayer and supplication, with thanksgiving, let your requests be made known to God; and the peace of God, which surpasses all understanding, will guard your hearts and minds through Christ Jesus." Philippians 4:19, 6-7

"When you lie down, you will not be afraid; Yes, you will lie down and your sleep will be sweet." Proverbs 3:24

"He will not let your foot slip. He who watches over you will not slumber." Psalms 121: 3 (NIV)

Sweet Dreams!

EPILOGUE

I love happy endings. As an avid reader, I enjoy suspense, surprise, adventure, and intriguing characters. I also love it when a story offers new ideas, or new ways of thinking about old ideas, and take-away values that stay with me long after the book has been closed.

I have noticed great endings often go back to the beginning and complete a circle of satisfaction for readers. I want this book to offer those qualities. So, let's go all the way back. The title itself suggests a summary, with help from Webster's Dictionary:

OVERCOME DEPRESSION:
STRATEGIES FROM SCIENCE & SCRIPTURE

Overcome Depression:

To overcome:

1. To get the better of in competition or struggle; to conquer.

2. To master, prevail over, or surmount; to overcome an obstacle.

We can agree depression is a struggle, a multi-layered problem, or obstacle. It may be less obvious, but equally valid, to think of it as a competition. The Apostle Paul did this when he compared his life and his mission to a race.

"...But none of these things move me; nor do I count my life dear to myself, so that I may finish my race with joy, and the ministry which I received from the Lord Jesus, to testify to the gospel of the grace of God." Acts 20: 24

Racing can be a simple child's game or a serious Olympic event. To compete in high-level competition requires dedicated training, relentless focus, and specialized tactics.

Sprints emphasize acceleration, and staying in one's own lane. Middle and Longer distance races need pacing and stamina. Relays require more observation, cooperation and alignment. Hurdlers also need coordination and rhythm to leap standard obstacles. Steeplechase sets a less predictable rhythm, demanding greater flexibility to clear more unique obstacles and hazards. Marathons shift the emphasis to endurance.

Life is our race, and we're all in it. We may find ourselves entered in multiple events as we press on towards the prize. One great and constant comfort is that our lane assignments, and particular challenges are known, and governed with love, by our Lord. He also promises help, and eventual, ultimate victory. We can choose how we run our race. This is your leg of our relay. Pass it on.

Strategies

As different racing styles require different tactics—so do our challenges in the race to overcome depression. Tactics are the strategies we need to apply. This text offers more than one hundred hands-on, practical, do-able strategies.

We looked for the 'So What' factors—and studied how they connect with brain science, and with scripture. We have also explored evidence-based cognitive therapies. We reviewed our need, and power, to check our thoughts, and to challenge those that are in error, or are unhelpful. Emotional Aikido was introduced as an alternative to the direct CBT challenge of 'thought-checking'.

We build recovery skills with strategies and support. That word 'with' also takes on special meaning for us. It's the opposite of 'without'. And, we are never alone, *without* the company and love of our Lord. This word also means that we don't have to meet challenges with empty hands, without resources.

I pray your discovery of these things sparks new hope, to free you from the grip of resignation and despair.

from Science:

I recently discovered the term Neuro-Theology. I love the way it describes the inter-relationship of human structures and functions, with heavenly intent.

Neurology is defined as a branch of medicine concerned especially with the structures, health and functions of the brain and nervous system. Theology is defined as the study of religious faith, practice and experience: The study of God and God's relationship to the world. The two can combine to powerful effect—for our benefit.

The sciences of psychology, social connections, of movements, nutrition and sleep, all add to, and inform, the choices we can make in determining how we will use the gifts we have within.

We are fearfully and wonderfully made, in the image of God. By His plan, we can become active partners in shaping and applying our abilities (including brain operations, and the structure itself) to more abundant living—starting here, and now.

I am excited to share amazing discoveries about operation of our whole, integrated systems. The more we learn about our divine design, and discover the powerful gifts we have within - the more we are able to recognize and appreciate our designer [God]. This is the training and conditioning we need to build endurance for our race.

And Scriptures:

'Scriptures' may be the last word in this title—but it's first in order of importance. The Word of God is our living standard of truth. It's that solid rock on which we can stand—and build our lives. I was inspired to share scripture in every chapter of this book because it enlightens every part of our learning process, and our recovery.

Cognitive Behavioral Therapy is effective. It requires us to check our thinking—and measure it by standards of truth and helpfulness. The Bible tells us that our hearts can deceive us—that we cannot always, fully and objectively see the truth of our own condition. In times of great stress or emotional struggle, that becomes more evident. And yet, that's when we need clarity the most to check and challenge our thinking. Thank God we have His word. Confusion reigns in the world, but we can't go wrong by aligning our thoughts with Scripture.

In scripture we find proofs of Love, Comfort, Peace, and Protection. We are assured that God is for us, and that our weakness does not condemn us. Instead, it serves as a perfect display for His strength. We believers can truly know that light has come into the world, and is shining—even when we feel lost in the dark. When we feel far from God, and can't find Him—He does know right where we are. We can hold on, because He is with us, and will never leave us. We are not alone.

If you don't know the assurance of those statements, may I invite you to join a life-changing conversation between yourself and God? The King of heaven loves you, wildly and passionately, just as you are. He wants you to know Him. It can begin with your open-hearted introduction—and include all of your toughest questions. I defined prayer as a conversation between two people who love each other. It can also be between our loving God, and one who is starting to consider the desirability of such a relationship. The invitation is yours. I pray that you will be blessed in acceptance.

Congratulations for reading all the way through to the end. A lot of information has been presented—in a short time. It'll take a while to digest. I have one more story to share, and it's important.

Patients in my recovery skills classes could easily feel over-whelmed, by too much information, and fears of a steep learning curve. I asked them: "If we, as a group, went to an all-you-can-eat (smorgasbord) buffet, and each of us took all we desired, of whatever we wanted—what are the odds that we would each return to the table with exactly the same selections, in exactly the same amounts?" They would not take any bets on those odds. Would you?

Now, I ask you to visualize the concepts, tips, and strategies in this book as a smorgasbord-type feast of ideas. As I assured my patients, I assure you: there is no rigid expectation that you memorize, or apply every strategy, 100% of the time. Only *you* can taste and see which ones serve your needs best. Load up on those. Remember, it's an all-you-can-eat buffet, so go back for second servings or to try different varieties as you wish.

I am so thankful for the privilege to have worked on this project and to share it with you. In these pages I have shared what I have been blessed to learn, as well as personal experiences. I have not mastered *all* of the strategies presented here—I'm still a work in progress, but I have found strength and help in the writing. I was inspired to write this book for you—and it ministered, to me. Thank you for joining me. We're in this together. I have two more scripture gems to share:

- 1 Peter 5:10 "The God of all grace who called you to His eternal glory in Christ, after you have suffered a little while, will Himself restore you and make you strong, firm and steadfast".

- Hebrews 12:1 [The Race of Faith] "Therefore we also, since we are surrounded by so great a cloud of witnesses, let us lay aside every weight, and the sin which so easily ensnares us, and let us run with endurance the race that is set before us."

In Chapter One, we spoke of winning the Daytona 500. Now, let's start those engines… and *drive-Baby-DRIVE*.

Blessings, Love and Laughter to you,
Marge

Visit me at www.margaretlalich.com.

Note: If you gained benefit from this book, please leave a review on the bookstore website where you purchased it. Thank you.

ACKNOWLEDGMENTS

This work has been a blessing and a passion. I owe thanks to many for its completion. First thanks and praise are due to my Lord Jesus Christ, who gave me the desire, inspiration, strength, ability, and opportunities to learn about, and to share the gifts that lay within.

I thank my best friend, the love of my life, and my partner forever, my husband Joe Lalich, for supporting my education and career development, and for believing enough, for both of us, that all things are possible. He did not survive cancer long enough to see this goal accomplished, but he certainly dreamed it with me.

Special thanks are due to Mary Weins, and Randall Haslam two of the brightest and best editing advisors I could have wished for. Without their multiple and patient readings, corrections, ideas, suggestions, and encouragement this work would never have attained the measure of clarity and coherence I hope you found in these pages. Their wit, wisdom, and generous labors of love helped keep me going, and kept me on track. I am blessed with these talented siblings, and I thank God for the love and encouragement of my entire family.

I am grateful for the friendships and lessons learned with colleagues at Napa State Hospital. I also thank the thousands of patients who shared with me. In teaching, I learned so much.

I owe thanks for support and counsel from Pastor, Bill Walden, Associate Pastor Vince and his wife (and my friend) Patty Asaro, as well as the family of believers at Cornerstone Ministry in Napa, CA.

I am grateful to the mentors and friends at Inspire Christian Writer's Group, and the Mt. Hermon Christian Writer's Conference—especially to Jan Kern (to whom that last ellipses is dedicated).

I have been blessed by the works of brilliant scientists, researchers, doctors, clinicians, and counselors, and by other personal heroes. They shined their lights on my paths of discovery. I am indebted to each listed in the bibliography, and more.

Finally, thank you, dear readers. You are last, but certainly not least on my list. Without your time and attention in reading this book, it would be meaningless.

Blessings, love, and laughter to you

BIBLIOGRAPHY

Amen, Daniel G./Routh, Lisa C., M.D. *Healing Anxiety And Depression*. Penguin Group USA, 2004.

Amen, Daniel G. *Healing the Hardware of the Soul: Enhance Your Brain to Improve Your work, Love and Spiritual Life*. Free Press, 2008.

American College of Sports Medicine. "ACSM's Guidelines for Exercise Testing and Prescription." Philadelphia: Lippincott Williams & Wilkins, 2000.

The AARP Bulletin (June 2018, page 42), cited "CareMore's hire of Chief Togetherness Officer."

Blumenthal, James A., Patrick J. Smith, and Benson M. Hoffman. "Is Exercise a Viable Treatment for Depression?" ACSM's health Health & Fitness Journal 16.4 (2012): 14-21. PMC. Web. 4 Sept. 2018.

Bombeck, Erma. *If Life Is a Bowl of Cherries, What Am I Doing In The Pits*, Fawcett Crest, 1985.

Bradshaw, Terry, and David Fisher. *Keep It Simple*. Pocket Books, 2003.

Brilliant, Ashley. I May *Not Be Totally Perfect, but Parts of Me Are Excellent*. Brilliant Enterprises (May 1997).

CDC: "9 Million Americans Use Prescription Sleeping Pills," AP August 30, 2013, NewYorkDailyNews.com/life-style/health.

Chris, et al. "14 Celebrities Who Have Experienced Depression." Everyday Health, Everyday Health, 4 Mar. 2016. www.everydayhealth.com/pictures/celebrities-who-have-experienced-depression/.

Cozolino, Louis. *The Neuroscience Of Psychotherapy: Healing The Social Brain, 2nd Ed.,* (p.7-8) 2010, W.W. Norton & Co., New York.

"Depressive Disorders." *Diagnostic and Statistical Manual of Mental Disorders, 5th. Edition,* doi: 10.1176/qppi.books .978089042 5596.807874.

Doidge, Norman. *The Brain That Changes Itself: Stories of Personal Triumph from the Frontiers of Brain Science.* Scribe Publications, 2009.

Doidge, Norman. *The Brains Way of Healing: Remarkable Discoveries and Recoveries from the Frontiers of Neuroplasticity.* Penguin Books, 2016.

Environmental Work Group. "EWG Shoppers Guide To Pesticides In Produce." EWG.org.

Frankl, Victor. *Man's Search for Meaning* Beacon Press; 4th edition, (March 30, 2000.).

Freund, B.J, Wade, C.E, Claybaugh, J.R "Effects of exercise Exercise on Atrial Natriuretic Factor. Release Mechanism and Implications for Fluid Homeostasis." Sports Med 1988, 6 364 376.

Geisler, Norman., and Frank Turek. *I Don't Have Enough Faith to Be an Atheist.* Good Seed Publishing, 2009.

Goodheart, Annette. *Laughter Therapy: How to Laugh about Every-thing in Your Life That Isn't Really Funny.* Less Stress Press, 1994.

Hallowell, Edward M. *Worry: Controlling It and Using It Wisely.* Pantheon, 1997.

Harris, Russ. *The Happiness Trap: Stop Struggling, Start Living.* Trumpeter, 2008.

Henslin, Earl Dr. *This Is Your Brain on Joy: A Revolutionary Pro-gram for Balancing Mood, Restoring Brain Health, and Nurturing Spiritual Growth.* Thomas Nelson, 2011.

Highnam,C.L., Bleile, K.M.; (2011) "Language in the Cerebellum." American Journal of Speech-Language Pathology Vol.20 337-347.

Holy Bible: New King James Version,: Containing the Old and New Testaments. : James Version, American Bible Society, 2010.

Holy Bible: New International Version, Zondervan, 2017.

Howard, Pierce J. *The Owner's Manual for the Brain: the Ultimate Guide to Peak Mental Performance at All Ages.* William Morrow, and Imprint of HarperCollins Publishers, 2014.

Hyman, Mark. *The Ultramind Solution: Fix Your Broken Brain by Healing Your Body First.* Simon & Schuster, 2010.

Hyman, Mark. *The Blood Sugar Solution Cookbook: More Than 175 Ultra-Tasty Recipes for Total Health and Weight Loss.* Little, Brown and Company, 2013.

Jessen NA, Munk ASF, Lundgaard I, Nedergaard M. "The Gglymphatic System: A Beginner's Guide." Neuro-chem Res. 2015:1-17.

Katz, Lawrence, et al. *Keep Your Brain Alive: 83 Neurobic Exercises to Help Prevent Memory Loss and Increase Mental Fitness.* Workman Publishing Company, 2014.

Keane, Bill. The Family Circus:. IDW Pub., 2009.

Ledoux, Joseph E., and Jack M. Gorman. "A Call To Action: Overcoming Anxiety Through Active Coping." American Journal of Psychiatry, vol. 158, no. 12,2001, pp.1953-1955., doi: 10,1176/ap-pi.aajp.158.12.1953.

Linehan, Marsha. "Three Approaches to Personality Disorders: Dialectical Behavioral Therapy." Psychotherapy.net, LLC, 2013.

McCarthy, Mike. "Jo Cox Commission Calls for 'Minister for Loneliness'." Sky News, 15 Dec. 2017, news.sky.com/story/jo-cox-commission-calls-for-minister-for-loneliness-11171060.

McMinn, Mark R. *Cognitive Therapy Techniques in Christian Counseling.* Wipf & Stock, 2007.

Perlmuter, David. *Brain Maker.* Yellow Kite, 2017.

Pert, Candace B. *Molecules of Emotion.* Pocket Books, 1997.

Perry, Hazard. "Famous Navy Quotes: Who Said Them and When." Naval History and Heritage Command. Archived from the original on September 23, 2007. Retrieved September 3, 2011.

Quote: "Dr. Seuss Quotes." BrainyQuote.com. Xplore Inc, 2018. Accessed 3 September 3, 2018. https://www.brainyquote.com/quotes/dr_seuss_106026.

Quote: "T. Boone Pickens Quotes." BrainyQuote.com. Xplore Inc., 2018. 3 Accessed September 3, 2018. https://www.brainyquote.com/quotes/t_boone_pickens_160506.

Ratey, John J., and Eric Hagerman. *Spark: The Revolutionary New Science of Exercise And The Brain.* Little, Brown, 2013.

Ratey, John. J. *A User's Guide To The Brain: Perception, Attention and The Four Theaters Of The Brain.* Abacus, 2007.

Reiner, Rob, et al. A Few Good Men.

Shukner, David. "Steven Hawking's Second Reith Lecture: Annotated Transcript". bbc.com/news/science-environment-35421439 (2 Feb. 2016).

Solomon, Gary. *Reel Therapy: How Movies Inspire You to Overcome Life's Problems.* Lebhar-Friedman Books, 2001.

Star Trek: A Beginner's Guide, Cover Story—American Film Institute Americanfilm.afi.com/issue/2013/4/cover-story

Taber, K.H. Ph.D., Redden, M., M.D., and Hurley, R., M.D.; "Functional Anatomy Of Humor: Positive Affect and Chronic Mental Illness." The Journal of Neuropsychiatry & Clinical Neurosciences 19: 358-362, November 2007.

Triveldi, M.H., Rush A.J., Wisniewski S.R., et al. "Evaluation of Outcomes With Citalopram For Depression Using Measurement-based Care In STAR*D: Implications For Clinical Practice." American Journal of Psychiatry.

Tipton, Charles M. "Medicine And Science In Sports And Exercise??? " 1984. Medicine & Science in Sports & Exercise, vol.16, no.1, 1984, p.1., doi:10.1249/00005768-198401000-00002.

URMC News: "Scientists Discover Previously Unknown Leaning System In The Brain," On-Line Journal: Science Translational Medicine, August 15, 2012.

United States Department of Agriculture. UsdaUSDA.gov.

Watkins, Alan. Coherence: The Secret Science of Brilliant Leadership. Kogan Page, 2014.

Xie L, Kang H, Xu Q, Chen MJ, Liao Y, et al. "Sleep drives Drives Metabolite Clearance from the Adult Brain." Science. 2013; 342(6156):373-77.

Yardley, Jonathan. "*Pogo Through the Wild Blue Wonder: The Complete Syndicated Comic Strips, Volume 1* by Walt Kelly." The Washington Post, 15 Jan. 2012.

ABOUT THE AUTHOR

Margaret Lalich is a believer, teacher, and author. She is also a Certified Laughter Leader. Her First love is her Lord—then family, friends and readers. She enjoyed a 31-year career as a clinician and educator, serving patients recovering from major mental illnesses. She hopes to help readers discover their gifts, and to increase their joy.

Margaret lives in Northern California, USA. Connect with her at www.margaretlalich.com.